£1.65
9A76

Abortion in Demand

'Abortion must be the key to a new world for women, not a bulwark for things as they are, economically nor biologically. Abortion should not be either a perquisite of the legal wife only, nor merely a last remedy against illegitimacy. It should be available for any woman, without insolent inquisitions, nor ruinous financial charges, nor tangles of red tape. For our bodies are our own.'

F.W. Stella Browne, 1935

Victoria Greenwood
and Jock Young

ABORTION IN DEMAND

with a foreword by
Peter J. Huntingford MD FRCOG

Pluto Press

First published 1976 by Pluto Press Limited
Unit 10 Spencer Court, 7 Chalcot Road
London NW1 8LH

Designed by Tom Sullivan
Cover designed by Penny Abrahams

Printed by Bristol Typesetting Company Limited
Barton Manor, St Philips, Bristol

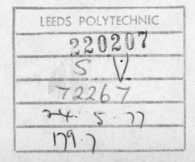

Contents

Tables

Acknowledgements

In the process of writing this book many people freely gave their time both in providing suggestions, criticisms and entertainment. We would particularly like to thank Juliet Ash, Pam Brighton, Judy Cottam, Sally Hesmondhalgh, Peter Huntingford, Chris Langford, Mary McIntosh, Frank Pearce, Colin Prescod, Sheila Rowbotham, Madeleine Simms and Dave Widgery. The staff of the Institute of Race Relations, and the National Abortion Campaign were most helpful; Jane Bowden typed the illegible manuscript and provided trenchant criticism; Nigel Fountain – what can one say – is the best sub-editor in the business. To both our households for uncomplainingly putting up with the turning of our homes into sweat shops during the writing of this book.

Victoria Greenwood
Jock Young
London, May 1976

Victoria Greenwood lectures in criminology at the Middlesex Polytechnic; is a committee member of the National Deviancy Symposium; and is currently writing *Crimes of Sex*, a study of prostitution, homosexuality, abortion and pornography.

Jock Young is Principal Lecturer in Sociology at the Middlesex Polytechnic; a founder member of the National Deviancy Symposium; and author of a number of books, including *The Drugtakers* (1971), *The New Criminology* (1973), *Media as Myth* (forthcoming).

Peter J. Huntingford, MD FRCOG, is Professor of Gynaecology in the University of London at the London Hospital and St Bartholomew's Hospital Medical Colleges.

Foreword

Originally a conservative, as a result of experience in dealing with women seeking contraception, abortion and sterilization, and through a greater awareness of reality, my views have changed to the extent that I now believe they should all be readily available as a right to every person without control by vested interests.

Discussions of contraception, abortion and sterilization cannot be divorced from their wider social context. It is generally not possible for women to exercise and enjoy their sexuality (as men have always done) independently of their reproductive role. Society resolves the conflict by assuming that the sexual drives of men and women are fundamentally different; that marriage and the family unit are essential to an ordered society; that most, if not all, women find fulfilment in motherhood; that infertility and childlessness bring unhappiness; that women who do not share these attitudes are, either totally or in part, not quite normal; that women who find themselves pregnant and reject the situation are irresponsible not to have foreseen and avoided the possibility; that the need for contraception can always be anticipated; that people can gain insight into their needs without ever regretting their actions; that present methods of contraception are satisfactory; that sexual drives remain stable throughout life; that prevention must be better than cure; and, therefore, that for everyone contraception must be preferable to abortion. I question all of these attitudes and assumptions.

Society is gradually recognizing that women should be able to exercise one or both of the two roles open to them – as a mother and/or as a member of society contributing on equal terms with men – without prejudice. But real choice between the options cannot exist until such time as the means for all women to choose freely are made available. Such means include : equal opportunities with men for education and employment; protection of employment during childbirth and motherhood; support for one-parent families; facilities for the day-care of children; flexible working hours; recognition that motherhood is an experience of life equivalent to uninterrupted employment; and ready access to all methods of fertility control.

The abortion debate provokes strong emotional reactions, none of which is particularly constructive. *Abortion in Demand* is a constructive attempt to provide historical and political perspective to one of the issues associated with the control of individual fertility and freedom. This book has provided me with insight, since it explains some of the reasons why I, as a male gynaecologist, have changed and why I now react as I do.

Many of my colleagues would like to separate medicine and politics. Many of them also believe that medical and social considerations can be distinguished. In discussions to do with human reproductive behaviour, nowhere is it more clear that boundaries between medicine, politics and the needs of society cannot be drawn. If exhortations to abstain and to recognize moral absolutes are ignored, the control of reproduction is almost exclusively dominated by the medical profession, who are generally unwilling to share their power or to consult the consumers of their skills. The reality that privileged people – the articulate, those who know the right people, and those with money or other favours to bestow – have always found it easy to divorce their sexual enjoyment from their reproductive capacity is ignored. Whilst the political and social import of such discrimination is denied or dismissed as irrelevant.

In the present state of technology we are not in sight of the perfect contraceptive – one that is cheap, easy to use, without risk, acceptable and readily available. If individuals – women as well as men – are to be able to control their own fertility in a socially responsible way and enjoy their sexuality for its own sake, safe abortion is essential. Safe abortion services could be provided in this country by the National Health Service now, if those responsible really cared and wished to do so. It is not the financial resources that are lacking, but the will to do so. Safe early abortion does not require admission to hospital, costly operating theatre time, or highly trained specialist surgeons. There are plenty of willing doctors (nurses and other people) who could be trained to perform early abortion with safety and skill. Instead of the cold, impersonal and intimidating hospitals, each community could be provided at relatively little cost with suitable homely and inviting premises. The cost of providing the required unlimited abortion services would be less than that of the restricted abortion facilities at present available under the NHS and in private.

It is shameful that we are not able to support one of the social services essential for the liberation of women from the role traditionally imposed upon them by our society. The NHS is accepting progressively less responsibility for the British women seeking abortion; intolerable regional variations exist in the ready availability of abortion; nearly everywhere women have to beg reluctant doctors to grant their request; and despite seeking abortion early in pregnancy far too many women experience unacceptable delays in obtaining abortion that increase the physical risks and emotional suffering. Abortion is not unlimited in this country, and never will be until those responsible for the health of society recognize political and social realities beyond the narrow confines of medical technology.

Peter J. Huntingford, MD FRCOG
London, May 1976

11

Introduction

In 1975 two massive demonstrations took place in London. One noisily chanted 'Not the Church, Not the State, Women Must Decide Their Fate'. The other sombrely bore the placards 'Abortion Kills'. The first represented the most significant show of strength by the women's movement. Its message was that abortion was a woman's right. Abortion law reform which up till that time had involved pressure group politics and parliamentary procedure was now a central issue mobilizing a wide spectrum of women. A dramatic change in attitude had taken place – abortion was now an unconditional demand on the state, the basic right of a woman to control her own fertility. The second demonstration could not have been a greater contrast. Church youth clubs, nuns with banners, the embittered middle aged and the sexually repressed young gathered together to fight 'this age of permissiveness' which they saw as symbolized in the legalisation of abortion.

The trigger for both demonstrations was the attempt by James White, Labour MP for Glasgow Pollock, to restrict the grounds for abortion. His Abortion Amendment Bill 1975 was seen as a tentative step in the right direction by the anti-abortionists (Society for the Protection of the Unborn Child, SPUC). For the pro-abortionists of the National Abortion Campaign (NAC) it was a ghastly reversal of existing gains.

Yet, despite the vigour of the abortion debate, there is surprisingly little analysis of the politics which underlie it. What analysis exists remains shallow and cursory. On the left it is often suggested, for example, that the proposed 1975 Amendment to the

13

Abortion Act was somehow a direct reflection of ruling class interests. Yet in 1967, at a time of relative affluence, high demand for labour and expanding social services, when to engage in measures which would limit the size of the population did not make economic sense, we had an Abortion Act which led to a vast expansion in the number of legal abortions. And, in 1975, confronted with a major recession, with a low demand for labour, high unemployment and massive cuts in the social services, the British parliament debated an Amendment to the 1967 Abortion Act which is popularly seen as involving a substantial reduction in the number of abortions. Other, more pragmatic governments have acted in precisely the opposite direction. Rumania having introduced permissive legislation in 1956, became alarmed at the rapid decline in the birth rate and its effect on labour supply. As a result in 1966 they introduced restrictive abortion legislation together with a number of pro-natalist policies, such as a bonus system for babies, in an attempt to raise the birth rate. Likewise, Japan, having introduced the Eugenic Protection Law in 1948 specifically to reduce the population, is now concerned to restrict abortion arguing that it is unnecessary in an era of prosperity.

From the opposing camp, a parallel reduction of the abortion issue to one of simple economic interests occurs. Here the financial gain of a small number of black sheep doctors is seen to have *caused* an expansion in the number of abortions. Yet it is anyone's bet whether this expansion has taken place, given that there has always been a substantial number of illegal abortions. The demand for abortion springs from the fundamental predicament of women – it is hardly likely to be affected by the few doctors touting for trade.

From another perspective abortion is viewed as a moral issue unrelated to economic interests. Like capital punishment, abortion is seen as a matter of conscience; a product of ethical or religious conviction. A current notion is that a small group of ideologically motivated men and women work to inflict on the public their moral convictions and achieve their aims by hood-

14

winking a sleeping parliament. A moral coup is accomplished and the general public left to face the consequences of the new legislation. On the one hand the Society for the Protection of the Unborn Child (SPUC) argues that the 1967 Act flew in the face of public opinion; on the other hand, the National Abortion Campaign (NAC) has seen the 1975 Amendment as the idiosyncratic ploy of James White, Leo Abse and a coterie of extreme right-wing Conservative MPs. Yet public opinion has scarcely ever in the last twenty years, both in attitudes and behaviour, been anti-abortion and the number of Labour MPs who back White make it more than just a question of White's idiosyncrasies.

Three major positions have emerged in the debate on abortion: SPUC argues for the total abolition of abortion except in a tiny minority of medical cases. The reformers, in contrast, are in general agreement with the spirit of the 1967 Abortion Act but are split into two hostile wings – the progressives who feel the Act has achieved its purpose and merely requires administrative adjustments; and the conservatives (like White) who consider that the spirit of the Act has been violated and would support stringent amendments in order to iron out its excesses. Both share the same reformist political philosophy: neither for example *oppose* abortion, but both oppose abortion *on demand*. Their differences lie in what they think are the permissible grounds for abortion and in how they interpret the effects of the legislation. Many of the people who supported the James White Amendment Bill could be classed as conservative reformers although the backbone of the Bill's support was clearly anti-abortionist. Finally there is the National Abortion Campaign (NAC) with its roots in the women's movement. It stands for abortion on demand.

The 1967 Act was the end result of thirty years' concerted reformist politics, channelled through the Abortion Law Reform Association (ALRA) in its role as a parliamentary pressure group and a major influence on public opinion. The 1960s could be characterized as an era of social reform. Legislation in the areas of juvenile delinquency, poverty, divorce, capital punishment, drug use, homosexuality and criminal justice came in for a radical re-appraisal (e.g. Murder/Abolition of the Death Penalty Act 1965, Sexual Reform Act 1967, Criminal Justice Act 1967, Divorce Reform Act 1969, Misuse of Drugs Act 1971). The political base for such a catalogue of reforms was the dominant bloc within the Labour Party which viewed a mixed economy as desirable and argued for state intervention backed by expert guidance. Problems abounded in society but these could be eliminated by selective social engineering and piecemeal reform.

The relative affluence of the 'sixties supported the view that there was no longer much difference between the working class and the middle class; that a classless society was emerging and that politics should concern itself with the supposedly shared interests of the vast majority, and should abandon sectional disputes. The working class was, in this view, firmly incorporated into the social contract: the mass of 'rational' individuals within society rejected class attitudes and perceived the social order as one of harmony and collective interest. Social problems existed either because of some government oversight or because of the unreasonableness of the individuals involved. As for those social problems that remained despite the rise in incomes and the slum clearance programmes they were segregated into three categories:

The first was made up from the *new poor*, chiefly the old, the structurally unemployed in areas of declining industries, and the handicapped. What needed doing was to integrate them into a 'caring' society.

The second category was formed by the *maladjusted*. Juvenile delinquency, female crime, or mental illness, could not, given the reformers' premises, be explained by poverty or perceived injustice (as they might have been in previous eras). They were aberrations, a product of factors unrelated to the failures of society a result of the personal inadequacies of the individuals concerned. Chief amongst the theories that evolved to cope with the problem was the maternal deprivation theory, associated with the work of John Bowlby. Its 'progressive' implication was that it was neces-

16

sary to treat – chiefly through specially manned state institutions – the unfortunate victims of maladjustment rather than punish the offender as the conservative 'law and order' campaigners would insist on doing. It called for the *recategorization* of the offender: from wilful culprit to sick victim. As in the case of the 'new poor', the problem of 'maladjustment' was to be admitted only if it involved small sections of the population and did not imply that there was anything wrong with society in general. That poverty, crime and mental illness were endemic throughout society was a fact which had to be ignored at all costs.

The last group were the *wrongly stigmatized*. Some social problems, chiefly in the area of sexual offences, were seen to be incorrectly treated as criminal. Homosexuals, prostitutes, juvenile sexual offenders and women seeking abortions were seen essentially as inadequates whose plight was made worse by state persecution. The task here was to *decriminalize* them. They too constituted a *marginal* problem within an essentially just society.

The reformist perspective on abortion fits well into these premises. Abortion is perceived as a peripheral problem involving either (a) those women who are medically unfit, or (b) those who are psychologically disturbed and to whom pregnancy and childbirth would precipitate further problems, or (c) those women from 'deprived' and 'demoralized' social backgrounds whose families are already of 'abnormal' size, or (d) those girls who are too young to act rationally in their sexual behaviour and are also incapable of bringing up a child. While it is true that women in these categories are in dire need of abortion facilities, a vast number of other women also have problems. The reformers neglect these women. They assume that only the fringes need facilities and that when other women demand abortion they are being frivolous.

1.
The 1967 Abortion Act

Abortion has always existed. Throughout history women have used various substances, objects and instruments which they hoped would result in an abortion.

Eskimos used carved walrus rib. In tenth century Persia women used sharpened marrow root. Herbal concoctions and chemical solutions provide the 'old wives' tales' of abortion in Britain. These and other methods have been widely (and successfully) used for thousands of years. Women have subjected themselves to the risks of lead, quinine, soap, penny royal and direct physical assaults on their abdomens. Many of these methods involved extreme risk. Some of the substances were lethal. Others seriously damaged the woman's or child's (if the abortion failed) health. Abortion, it seems, has lasted as long as pregnancy itself.

In British common law, abortion prior to 'quickening', when the soul was presumed to enter the foetus, was not a crime, while abortion after quickening was a misdemeanour. Quickening occurred around the twelfth week, although the actual date of occurrence depended on the evidence of the woman who risked 'heavenly punishment' were she to lie.

The law changed in 1803, and abortion became a criminal offence. Quickening was still taken into consideration. The punishment for abortion before quickening was transportation, whipping, or imprisonment. After it the punishment was death.

Thirty-five years later the distinction was abolished along with the death penalty. In 1861 the Offences Against the Person

Act, Section 58, made abortion a misdemeanour. Anyone, including the woman herself, procuring an abortion could be sentenced to life imprisonment. Section 59 made it a misdemeanour punishable with imprisonment for three years to supply any instrument, poison or noxious thing for an abortion.

This Act formed the backbone of abortion legislation for the next one hundred years. However, it made no provision for termination of pregnancy on *medical* grounds. As medical techniques progressed it became accepted practice to carry out an abortion if it was thought necessary to save a woman's life.

In 1929 the Infant Life Preservation Act protected this practice. It stated that termination of pregnancy is unlawful except when the act has been proved to have been done in good faith to preserve the life of the mother. This also applied to the termination of a viable foetus. It thus posed ethical and moral questions about the status of abortion, the certainty of the law, and the viability of the foetus.

Since the early 1900s feminists and socialists have been campaigning for birth control and abortion. In an age when sex, birth control and abortion were taboo subjects women campaigned throughout the country for the right to control their own fertility. The first battles were over birth control, but by the 1930s support was growing for abortion law reform.

The main concerns of the agitation were the suffering of women who had to resort to backstreet abortions, and the legal penalties which made doctors reluctant to terminate pregnancies. But more radical ideas were being put forward too. In particular Stella Browne, a founder member of the Communist Party and a forerunner in the 1920s of the present abortion campaign argued consistently for abortion as a woman's *right*.

A case brought in 1938 against Alec Bourne, a consultant obstetrician, was expected to clear up the confusions arising from the 1929 Act. He had performed an abortion on a fourteen year old victim of a multiple rape – and invited the Attorney General to prosecute. The result was a liberal interpretation of the 1929 Act by Justice McNaughton which passed into English case law. It indicated that in certain circumstances a doctor had not only the right, but the duty to terminate pregnancy. It was lawful not only to save life, but also to safeguard the woman's health and to prevent her becoming, in his words, a 'physical or mental wreck'.

Bourne was acquitted and a legal precedent set. But far from clarifying the law the judgement increased the legal uncertainties and, furthermore, led to even greater inequality in the availability of abortions.

A minority of doctors began to interpret the 1929 Act liberally. They operated when they felt 'in good faith' that the 'mental or physical health of the patient was at risk'. The problem of proving the contrary lay with the prosecution. Doctors used their discretion in interpreting the law and the practice of 'therapeutic abortions' began to grow.

By 1961 about 2,300 abortions a year were taking place in the NHS. The number rose to 9,700 in 1967. [C.Tietze and D.Dawson, 1974, p.14.] The market for private abortions also expanded. At least 10,000 a year took place prior to 1968 in that sector. Legal ambiguities apparently diminished with the noise of a cash register, and the number of 'discreetly legal' operations undoubtedly went far beyond the original intentions of the judges.

Estimates of illegal abortion in Britain before 1967 vary from 15,000 to 100,000. The figures are questionable but all sides in the debate use them to measure the limits and restrictions of abortion legislation.

By the early 1960s, the law clearly had little support. Large numbers of semi-legal and illegal abortions were taking place. The existence of the private sector demonstrated that existing abortion legislation applied largely to those without means: 'abortion is like equal pay, the women who are best off get it'.

By then there had already been stringent attempts, partly inspired by the persistent pressure of ALRA on MPs, to rationalize and extend abortion facilities. Joseph Reeves in 1953, Kenneth Robinson in 1961, Renée Short in 1965 and Simon Wingfield

21

Digby in 1966 – all unsuccessfully introduced private members' abortion bills.

The first sign of real progress was Lord Silkin's two bills. The first was introduced in 1965, and laid the foundations for a thorough debate between the supporters and opponents of abortion. The reasons for women seeking abortions, the personal and social consequences of abortion, questions about medical freedom, the limits and extent of socio-medical decisions, the ethics and morality of legalizing abortion – topics which were to be returned to again and again in the ensuing years – were given an extensive and radical airing.

Silkin's intention was to legalize existing practices, to give legislative backing to therapeutic abortion. It was proposed that the McNaughton judgement become statute, and that both medical and social indications be permissible in allowing abortions.

Clause (1) would permit abortion, in good faith, by one medical practitioner 'in the belief that if the pregnancy were allowed to continue there would be grave risk of the patient's death or of serious injury to her physical or mental health resulting either from giving birth to the child or from the strain of caring for it'.

The clause included the restrictive and legally ambiguous concepts of 'grave' and 'serious', but this was balanced by social indications. These were further strengthened by the contentious clause (c) which legalized the termination of pregnancy by a registered medical practitioner 'in the belief that the health of the patient or the social conditions in which she is living (including the social conditions of her existing children) make her unsuitable to assume the legal and moral responsibility for caring for a child or another child as the case may be'. Abortion was seen as a means of ensuring social responsibility, of maintaining a stable family structure, and minimizing the number of inadequates, delinquents, deprived and depraved. Clause (c) admitted blatantly that existing social structures are inadequate, that social conditions are not always conducive to the up-bringing of well-adjusted, responsible citizens.

22

Criticisms and the debate on the clause revealed many of the prime interests and concerns of those involved in the business of abortion. The professional interests and ideology of the medical profession dominated, as discussions centred on the idea of 'good faith', on the status and numbers of doctors to be involved in the abortion decision and on the potentially radical principle that abortion be considered normal medical practice and not treated differently from other operations. The reformers' principles became evident in the debate as Lord Silkin made explicit where he thought 'social conditions' tied in with medical decisions:

> There are women who suffer from illnesses which, while they do not affect the pregnancy itself and therefore are not covered by paragraph (a), will nevertheless make her less able to bear the burdens of motherhood. Epilepsy is one case; a woman can be epileptic and nevertheless be otherwise quite capable physically and mentally of bearing a child. There is the case of the woman who is in prison, serving a long term commencing between the beginning of the pregnancy and the time at which she will give birth. Obviously that woman is inadequate to be a mother of a child. There is the persistent offender, or the shop-lifter, and there is the mother who has in the past been found guilty of neglecting or ill-treatment of her existing children. These are some of the cases I have in mind. There is the drug taker or the alcoholic. I am sure the right reverend Prelate (the Bishop of Exeter) would not suggest that such a mother is a fit person to be in charge of children. There is the woman who already has a large family, perhaps six or seven children . . . There is the question of the woman who loses her husband during pregnancy and has to go out to work, and obviously cannot bear the strain of doing a full day's work and looking after a child. There is the woman whose husband is a drunkard or a ne'er-do-well, or is in prison serving a long term, and she has to go to work. These are the cases I have in mind. [K.Hindell and M.Simms, 1971, pp.149-150.]

That these people were the intended targets of new legislation, was not to be forgotten.

It is interesting to note Lady Wootton's opposition to the Silkin Bill, her potentially radical statements often revealing a taste of the future. Lady Wootton was a notable Fabian socialist, feminist, and agnostic. She vehemently attacked the concept of the inadequate mother (the amended clause (c)) constituting grounds for abortion, commenting 'It could indeed be the beginning of Nazi racialism'. Wootton was worried by the eugenic undertones of the Bill and by the dumping of social matters into the hands of the medical profession. She wrote to Lord Silkin: 'I have known too many Tory doctors who really think that the "lower classes" ought not to be allowed to reproduce themselves, though of course they would not put it like that.'

Concessions, restrictions, amendments and modifications wrecked much of Silkin's first Bill but the area of debate had been mapped. ALRA was confident that legislation on abortion was to follow soon. The second Silkin Bill was dropped and attention turned to a Private Member's Bill in the more important setting of the House of Commons.

ALRA had been the backbone of support in all the battles for new abortion legislation. Their humanitarian and reformist concerns for 'rightness, necessity and justice' formed the cornerstone of the Medical Termination of Pregnancy Bill, introduced by Liberal MP David Steel in 1966, Steel's concerns were the 15,000-100,000 illegal abortions per year and the farce of a law which discriminated about abortion in the NHS yet gave abortion on demand in the private sector.

The reforming concerns of the Bill's sponsors were clear from the start. Abortion should be available in instances of 'severe social hardship' – 'I think we must bear in mind some of the cases which are on the borderline between social, economic cases and purely medical cases' (Steel). Legislation however was to be restrictive: 'We want to stamp out the back street abortions but it is not the intention of the promoters of the Bill to leave a wide open door for abortion on demand.' For Steel, abortion should not be classed with having your tonsils out, and it was not a matter purely for women to decide.

The Medical Termination of Pregnancy Bill 1966:

1. (1) Subject to the provisions of this section a person shall not be guilty of an offence under the law relating to abortion when a preg-

nancy is terminated by a registered medical practitioner if that practitioner and another registered medical practitioner are of the opinion, formed in good faith –

(a) that the continuance of the pregnancy would involve serious risk to the life of or grave injury to the health, whether physical or mental, of the pregnant woman whether before, at or after the birth of the child; or

(b) that there is a substantial risk that if the child were born it would suffer from such physical or mental abnormalities as to be seriously handicapped; or

(c) that the pregnant woman's capacity as a mother will be severely overstrained by the care of a child or of another child as the case may be; or

(d) that the pregnant woman is a defective or became pregnant while under the age of sixteen or became pregnant as a result of rape.

(2) Except as provided by subsection (3) of this section, any treatment for the termination of pregnancy must be carried out in a hospital vested in the Minister of Health or the Secretary of State for Scotland under the National Health Service Acts, or in a registered nursing home, or in a place for the time being approved for the purposes of this section by the Minister or the Secretary of State.

(3) Subsection (2) of this section, and so much of sub-section (1) as relates to the opinion of another registered medical practitioner, shall not apply to the termination of a pregnancy by a registered medical practitioner in a case where he is of the opinion, formed in good faith, that the termination is immediately necessary in order to save the life of the pregnant woman.

(4) A termination of pregnancy performed on the ground of rape shall require the certificate of a registered medical practitioner consulted by the patient freshly after the alleged assault that there was then medical evidence of sexual assault upon her.

(5) A termination of pregnancy performed upon a girl under the age of sixteen shall require her express consent in addition to any necessary consent of her parent or guardian. [K.Hindell and M.Simms, 1971, Appendix 1, pp.245-246.]

In principle, reform was accepted by the majority of participants in the debate that followed. The big issue was how liberal or restrictive the legislation should be. The problem for the reformers was to make abortion available to certain categories of women without allowing women to 'degenerate into free-for-alls with the sleazy comfort of knowing' (J.Knight MP).

The social clause (c) was therefore the focus of debate. Steel admitted concern that the clause went beyond what the sponsors themselves had intended and might open the door to abortions of convenience. However a clause which allowed abortion to the deserving cases was important, for, as Roy Jenkins commented in describing the government's 'benevolent neutrality' to the Bill, clause 1(c) was 'an attempt to deal with a real issue'.

The rhetoric of reformism infused the entire debate. Those who accepted the social clause, saw it as helping maintain the family through avoiding overcrowding, poverty and deprivation. The majority opposing the social clause were alarmed that social problems should be papered over by so extreme a measure as abortion. Contraception and sterilization were surely more humane responses. Those concerned with the 'excesses' and racketeering were sceptical whether 'the right cure for social abuse is to legalize it with suitable restraints' (W.Deedes MP) – experience with gambling legislation had not proved the point.

The arena of argument made the objections of the medical profession (the Royal College of Obstetricians and Gynaecologists, RCOG, and the British Medical Association, BMA) and the Church of England important. The professional and status concerns of the medical establishment have been evident throughout the abortion debate; abortion remains for them primarily a medical issue, which would maintain their time-honoured monopoly of diagnosis and treatment. Their objections expressed concern that clause 1(c) represented non-medical criteria and would lead to 'excessive demand for termination on social grounds and this is unacceptable to the medical profession' (BMA). The central issue for them was 'medical freedom'. They saw a possible threat to independent clinical judgement, to their freedom 'to act in what they consider to be the best interests of each individual patient'.

The attitude of much of the medical profession, in particular the conservative RCOG, was epitomized by the reported remark of Professor McClaren: 'I do not think we should be asked to cut out social problems with a surgeon's knife.' [A.Hordern, 1971, p.122.]

The medical hierarchy's concern was one-sided. They were less worried about freedom for liberal doctors. They feared that doctors *opposed* to abortion might be pressured into terminating pregnancies. Paradoxically it was the reformers defending abortion who were to uphold clinical freedom and thus ensure that abortion remain primarily a medical decision.

Steel expressed concern that his Bill might go further than he intended and was open to the considerable influence of the BMA and RCOG, particularly since a RCOG report had warned that gynaecologists would not apply new legislation they opposed: 'legislators should be reasonably sure of their co-operation before deciding on any alteration of the Law.' [K.Hindell and M.Simms, 1971, p.168.] Acknowledging the influence of the medical profession, Steel amended his Bill in committee: the social clause was hopelessly weakened and restrictive legislation guaranteed.

The amendment removed clauses (c) and (d). A compromise was reached by widening the terms of permissible abortion under clause 1(a). The words 'grave and serious' were dismissed as legally dubious and replaced by the vaguer concepts of 'well-being' and 'total environment, actual or reasonably foreseeable'.

> Steel explained that his purpose in making these changes was not to remove social factors from the Bill but to make them part and parcel of a correct medical judgement, a judgement which would involve physical, mental and social factors concurrently. [K.Hindell and M.Simms, 1971, p.183.]

The compromise was necessarily vague, for it would allow individuals to interpret the Act to suit their own predilections. And Steel was later to be hoist by his own petard. ALRA although dismayed, supported the concession, because a 'social element' was retained.

When the Bill reached its final hearing in the Commons, the debate was lengthy, heated and vociferous.

When a small band of people tried to 'talk it out' the Labour government of the day made certain of its passage by giving as much extra parliamentary time as was necessary – a rare concession indeed for a Private Member's Bill. [D.Beazley and J.Knight, 1974.]

The Bill was approved and passed to the upper house. There a significant amendment was accepted which has been important subsequently and during the present backlash to the 1967 Act. At issue was the definition of 'risk'. Did it have to be, 'substantial', 'grave' or 'serious'? Lord Parker argued for balance, which could be achieved by the addition of the word 'greater'. So abortion would be legal if the risk to life or the risk of injury to health were *greater* by continuing pregnancy than by termination. (Throughout the debate abortion had been seen as 'dangerous'. It was assumed that in general the risk to life *from* abortion was greater than if a pregnancy continued.) This was seen as an adequate safeguard and accepted.

The Roman Catholic Tory MP, Norman St John-Stevas, astutely pointed out that if in time abortion should become safe, then it would be legally justified in *all* cases. This is just what happened. The reformers had created the loophole for 'abuse'.

After months of debate and modifications the Act received Royal Assent on 27 October 1967. It was not seen as the ultimate solution to the abortion problem. The need for constant review of the Act's workings was stressed. Some even hinted that after a number of years it should be repealed. The impact and consequences of the Act were to be scrutinized from the start.

The supporters of the 1967 Act were concerned to 'stamp out the scourge of criminal abortions' (Steel), to clear up the law and to change the situation which allowed abortion on demand for those with money. 'Excesses' were to go and some existing illegal categories were legalized.

It was a tidying-up operation, not an invitation to an abortion 'paradise'. The prevailing attitude was well expressed by the then Labour Health Minister, Kenneth Robinson. He denied the need for increased facilities. The beds that had been used for the

28

results of illegal abortion would from then on be used for legal terminations.

So the government was caught unprepared for the subsequent demand. 'Its immediate impact was greater even than its supporters had anticipated' wrote Keith Hindell and Madeleine Simms. In the first three years abortions rose from 35,000 to 87,000. By 1971 there were 95,000 legal abortions on British residents, 57 per cent in the NHS. Madeleine Simms again: 'In the NHS alone, nine times as many abortions were carried out in 1971, compared with five years earlier'. [Simms, 1972, 'Abortion and liberation', p.3.]

It is easy to see how the reformers failed to achieve their aims, by looking at the Act in detail:

1. (1) Subject to the provisions of this section, a person shall not be guilty of an offence under the law relating to abortion when a pregnancy is terminated by a registered medical practitioner if two registered medical practitioners are of the opinion, formed in good faith –
(a) that the continuance of the pregnancy would involve risk to the life of the pregnant woman, or of injury to the physical or mental health of the pregnant woman or any existing children of her family, greater than if the pregnancy were terminated; or
(b) that there is a substantial risk that if the child were born it would suffer from such physical or mental abnormalities as to be seriously handicapped.
(2) In determining whether the continuance of a pregnancy would involve such risk of injury to health as is mentioned in paragraph (a) of subsection (1) of this section, account may be taken of the pregnant woman's actual or reasonably foreseeable environment.
(3) Except as provided by subsection (4) of this section, any treatment for the termination of pregnancy must be carried out in a hospital vested in the Minister of Health or the Secretary of State under the National Health Service Acts, or in a place for the time being approved for the purposes of this section by the said Minister or Secretary of State.
(4) Subsection (3) of this section, and so much of subsection (1) as relates to the opinion of two registered medical practitioners, shall not apply to the termination of a pregnancy by a registered medical practitioner in a case where he is of the opinion, formed in good faith, that the termination is immediately necessary to save the life

or to prevent grave permanent injury to the physical or mental health of the pregnant woman. [*Abortion Act 1967*, Chapter 87.]

Clause 1 established clearly the importance of the medical practitioner. An abortion could not be carried out without the consent of two medical practitioners.

Since a woman requesting an abortion has *already* diagnosed her condition and is merely asking the doctor to act in the role of technician, she defies the traditional doctor-patient relationship. The medical profession were aware of this threat to their professional status. They were concerned to stress that it was for them to decide what they should do after they had determined what *they* thought were the patient's best interests. The result was that under the new Act a woman seeking abortion was at the mercy of the personal viewpoints of both GPs and consultants. A doctor refusing a termination was protected by the 'conscience clause' which served to clear him (as it often is) from all responsibility.

The power of the medical profession over abortion has significantly affected both the number of abortions, the techniques used and the route taken to them.

Before the Act GPs were inhibited from recommending women for abortions or carrying out clandestine illegal operations. Now they were permitted to exercise their medical judgement in accordance with their sympathies. Unlike gynaecologists who neither face, nor are aware of, the result of a decision not to terminate a pregnancy, GPs have to deal with the repercussions of a dangerous and illegal abortion, or with the resentful mother, with an unwanted child, and all the attendant problems. The local GP faces the lasting repercussions of refusal.

It was hardly surprising that GPs who had always been sympathetic to the case for abortion, began interpreting the Act liberally, disproving the notion that medical practices on abortion would remain unaltered. The RCOG were dismayed and amazed as the oft-quoted article by Mr T.L.T.Lewis, FRCS shows:

All in all, we (in the RCOG) did not expect a very great change in practice from that obtaining before the Act . . . How wrong we were. I'm afraid we did not allow for the attitude of firstly the general public, and secondly the general practitioners. [T.L.T.Lewis, 1969, pp.241-242.]

The increased demand for abortions cannot be explained merely by a shift from the illegal to the legal sector. Experience shows that wherever legislation has become more permissive, there has been an initial and generally sustained rise in the number of legal abortions. Easier access and acceptance of abortions enables many women who would not have risked the back street market, to terminate their pregnancies. Besides, the decision to abort is all the more 'attractive' when a society lacks the facilities and relationships which make a genuine choice to bring up a child practicable.

There is another side to the coin. Doctors with deep-seated anti-abortion views are also free to exercise their moral scruples. 'The doctor in refusing to terminate a pregnancy absolves himself from all responsibility', says the conscientous objection clause (sec 4, 1967 Act). 'No person shall be under any duty, whether by contract or by any statutory or other legal requirement, to participate in any treatment authorized by this Act to which he has a conscientious objection.'

As a result, Leeds gynaecologists could state in good faith in May 1967:

We, gynaecologists in the Leeds region, wish to state that should the Bill become law, our present practice of terminating pregnancies where well-established medical indications exist will be unchanged and we do not expect to terminate more pregnancies than before. [ALRA, *Evidence to the Lane Committee*, 1972.]

Such attitudes have resulted in immense discrepancies in the availability of abortions. In 1974 there were 13 NHS abortions to every 100 live births in Newcastle; 12 to 100 in London, whereas in Birmingham there were only four NHS abortions to every 100 live births. Area discrepancies frequently reflect the attitudes of the consultants who wield the power of ultimate decision. In Newcastle one consultant has been closely associated with ALRA,

31

whereas the leading consultants in Birmingham are conspicuous members of SPUC.

Wide discrepancies in resources also increase the problem: Newcastle, for instance, not only has more gynaecological beds per given population than Sheffield, but it also has twice as many consultant gynaecologists. These unjust differences have led to the growth of a large private/charitable sector to cater for the 'deficiency areas'. Unable to get an abortion on the NHS women go to the private sector, not out of choice, but out of necessity.

A further factor aided both a liberal interpretation of the Act and the expansion of a private sector. Clause 1(a) of the 1967 Act permitted abortion where:

> The continuance of the pregnancy would involve risk to the life of the pregnant woman, or of injury to the physical or mental health of the pregnant woman or any existing children of her family, greater than if the pregnancy were terminated.

In 1967, it was assumed that giving birth to a child was safer than having an abortion. The medical profession frequently said that abortion under the best of conditions, carried out with the best skill available, was a very dangerous operation. In this way they stressed the indispensability of their professional skills and supported their arguments about *their* concern for what is best for *their* patients. The claim was dubious even then. Lay abortions have always occurred, and a proportion of these have not involved hospitalization or danger. Further, even a superficial look at abortion statistics in countries like Hungary or Japan shows that liberal abortion laws plus mass facilities result in earlier terminations, advances in medical techniques, and a lowering of risks.

The claim is even more dubious now. In 1970 the legal abortion mortality rate was 13 per 100,000 – lower than the maternal mortality rate. Between 1968 and 1970 only two deaths were attributed to abortions performed in the thirteenth week – a mortality risk of 2 per 100,000 abortions, about one tenth of the maternal mortality risk. Although deaths from abortion after 12 weeks are higher in number, they still amount to less than the maternal mortality rate, and, moreover, are often undertaken as a result of the weakness of the Act.

The concept of 'greater risk' allowed comparison, and as medical techniques improved the logic of restraint turned on its own head, and a liberal interpretation of the Act was encouraged. Bitter irony though it be for the opponents of liberalization who had insisted on their phrase 'greater risk', it is *safer* to carry out an abortion, than to risk 'the continuance of pregnancy'.

The opportunity for a liberal interpretation of risk has led to the accusation that the law is tantamount to abortion on demand. This is incorrect, so long as abortions remain under the aegis of the medical profession. But for a section of the population this loophole in the 1967 Act allowed a much greater degree of liberalization than was ever intended. It has been argued that such permissive legislation makes it 'unlikely . . . that any prosecution will in future be brought against a doctor who observes the ostensible requirements of the Abortion Act. The danger now lies in those cases where a doctor refuses a demand to perform an abortion.' [R.A.G.O'Brien cited in D.Callahan, 1970, p.148.]

The reformers had succeeded in confounding their own aims. They wished to restrict abortion to the deserving and specified 'social grounds' to prevent abortion on demand. In practice they succeeded in loosening the general constraints on abortion and so provided their critics with substance for the accusation that they had permitted the thin end of the wedge of 'abortion on demand' to be created.

A further unintended consequence of the abortion law was the growth of abortion-consciousness. Women who previously had resorted to criminal or quasi-legal abortions, or given birth only to have their child adopted, or reluctantly accepted an unwanted child, were quick to avail themselves of a legal service. For many, abortions moved from the realm of a secret to a socially acceptable act.

In response to demand, and given the lack of NHS facilities, private and charitable clinics were rapidly established. Information bureaux widely advertised their services. The proportion of abortions occurring under the Health Service declined until, between 1972 and 1974, abortions on residents were evenly distributed between the private and public sectors.

Where supply does not meet demand, women with the know-how and money manipulate the market to buy the service. The result was that abortion facilities became available to precisely those 'normal' women with whom the Act was not primarily concerned – the well-off, educated and informed. Unable often to get abortions in the public sector (in 1972, 78 per cent of Pregnancy Advisory Service (PAS) patients were direct referrals from their doctors), these women constitute a large proportion of the clientele of the private/charitable sector.

For most of them it was not a privilege:

a 'free market' does not exist in abortions. A patient choosing to go privately is forced by law to go to one of the licensed nursing homes. Secondly, she has little time to 'shop around' for the lowest priced clinic and doctors. Thirdly, a patient is unlikely to question the charge publicly because of the peculiarly confidential nature of this operation. [V.Greenwood, 1973, p.46.]

These women are easy prey to the profit motive; extortionate sums can be levied from them; touting, rackets and exploitation can abound. Scandals steal the headlines and undoubtedly some doctors made inordinate sums of money in private abortion practice, as they have always done in the surgeries of Harley Street. Since the 1967 Act specified supervision and control of private clinics (sec. 1, clause 3), but did not regulate prices, it helped to promote the abuses for which it is now attacked.

Again the 1967 Act confounded its aims, in that far from wiping out inequalities in access to abortion, it has been party to their continuance and expansion. A sample of 1,000 PAS patients in 1972 showed that 73 per cent were single – the largest group being in the 20-24 age range – and only 35 per cent of the married sample had three or more children. As it turned out abortion was not the solution to problems of poverty, overcrowding and deprivation; it was more frequently a choice available to 'normal' women with whom the Act was not concerned.

The private/charitable market was also the sole provider of abortions to foreign women. In 1974, 54,000 foreign women had abortions in Britain, all of them in the private/charitable sector. Although no significant number of non-residents has ever obtained NHS abortions, the anti-abortionists latched on to this influx as a peculiarly obnoxious result of the Act.

That women are forced to travel hundreds of miles to a foreign country in order to seek medical assistance is, of course, lamentable. But it occurs precisely because of the pernicious laws in their countries of origin, laws which the anti-abortionists seek to emulate. Presumably they would wish British women to be similarly forced into such lengthy journeys and inconvenience.

The private sector of medicine has always profited from foreign clients. Yet it was not such profits or clientele that the anti-abortionists complained about, but that the business was abortion.

2.
The Consequences of the 1967 Abortion Act

By 1971, many of the failures of the 1967 Act were apparent. It had never been envisaged that the 1967 Act would close the abortion debate and both reformers and anti-abortionists were quick to use whatever evidence they could find to back up their arguments.

A flow of stories in the press since 1967, mostly about foreign women, touting, allegedly crooked clinics, and bribery had helped keep the subject alive. Half-truths, exaggerations and distortions abounded. A story in the papers on 2 July 1969 describing how thousands (one paper said thirty thousand) Danish women were coming on organized trips to the 'abortion capital of the world' for an inclusive fee of £120. Richard Crossman was asked in the House of Commons to confirm the story. He revealed that 46 Danish women had obtained abortions in Britain that year.

Such stories served to alert the public and, more importantly, parliament to malpractices and abuses of the Act. Fears and doubts expressed in the 1967 debate were seen to be real – abortion figures were constantly rising and rackets and exploitation appeared prevalent. The abuses existed for pro- and anti-abortionists alike. From their different perspectives they saw the necessity for changes, modifications and remedies.

ALRA was fairly content with the 1967 Act. It marked a more humane and liberal attitude to abortion. Although abuses and malpractices occurred they were practical problems that stood outside the realm of the law. True some deserving women who required abortions were not receiving them. But this was due to the lack of facilities, medical attitudes and occasionally to the timidity of women who still hesitated to consult their doctors.

The bias and prejudices of the medical profession were seen to be the main obstacles, and remedies lay in technical measures such as reorganizing staff and facilities within the Health Service, creating more facilities and better contraception and sterilization services. The ALRA *Newsletter* in 1968 summed up the situation:

> It is no longer the law that is preventing women obtaining NHS abortions, it is the attitude of some of the doctors and the shortage of NHS facilities. A further reform of the law will not alter these factors in the slightest. [ALRA *Newsletter* no.22, Autumn 1968.]

They believed that there were 100,000 illegal abortions prior to the Act, and their concern was that the law would just legalize existing practices. They showed no surprise at the rising number of recorded abortions. It was indeed possible that a number of illegal abortions were still occurring, due to regional discrepancies, doctors' attitudes and lack of facilities. But the remedy did not lie in further liberalization of the law but in technical solutions.

For ALRA the 1967 Act was a victory. It made abortions available to those desperate and deserving cases without allowing widespread abortion on demand. All that was now required were minor technical improvements. Thus Hindell and Simms write:

> After thirty four years ALRA looked forward to its own dissolution, and to the establishment of a more broadly based movement that would campaign, not only for the wider availability of abortion, but for better birth control and sterilisation facilities as well. [K.Hindell and M.Simms, 1971, p.225.]

The anti-abortionists, however, perceived the 1967 Act as a disaster. All their fears, concerns and doubts appeared to be confirmed. The Act, they argued, had not only opened the the door to free abortion on demand, but was tainted with criminality – abuses and excesses were its consequences.

The anti-abortionists did not have to rely solely on moral and ethical arguments. Statistics and scandals could now be paraded. Airy debates could now be supplemented by facts. The critics could turn the reformist arguments for the 1967 Act against the Act itself.

They put out powerful, emotive and ruthless propaganda deploring the Act. They (particularly SPUC) organized themselves into a powerful political lobby with wide public support. They set about increasing that support and, significantly, influencing the conservative wing of the reformers. In both they were highly successful.

By posing abortion as a moral issue, above political party and class, they have won backing from those who see the current economic recession and social and political crisis as a natural outcome of a liberal and permissive era imposed on the nation by selfish, ruthless minorities. Social order and stability can be restored only by reasserting traditional ideas of morality, authority, discipline, sexuality and the family.

At the same time they appealed to less reactionary people by appearing to take up the cause of the weak and powerless, arguing for 'social care, not abortion' (SPUC), for improved housing, family allowances and better social service provisions.

There was one snag to this campaign – the anti-abortionists could not openly call for contraception without breaking the backbone of their support within the Catholic Church. It was a weakness which reflects the fact that they had lost the battle over free contraception in the 'sixties, and were focusing on abortion as a second line of defence.

As they see it abortion is an open invitation for murder and a decline into an inhuman, brutal and uncivilized nation. 'History will show', wrote Malcolm Muggeridge,

whether such changes in our moral attitudes result as you believe in a more compassionate society, or as I believe represent a process of autogenocide arising out of the collective death wish of a spent bourgeoisie. [Letter to the *Guardian*, 3 April 1973.]

The anti-abortionists organized opposition to the Act from the start. Two attempts to amend it occurred in the first seven months of the Act, and in February 1970 a Conservative MP,

38

Bryant Godman Irvine, succeeded in tabling a private member's bill to restrict abortion. Recognizing possible defeat, and hoping that a Conservative government would provide a surer path to amendment, the opponents of reform 'talked out' their own bill.

SPUC and its associates continued to press for restrictions and bombard MPs with their propaganda. They succeeded with many of the Conservative MPs, some from the Labour Party, and gained support from prominent members of the medical profession. With the return of the Conservatives in 1970, they adopted a new strategy. In August 1970 they tabled a motion urging an inquiry into the Abortion Act. In 1971 Sir Keith Joseph gave in to the demand and established the Lane Committee.

The Lane Committee was given a limited brief: 'The Enquiry will be concerned with the way the Act is working and not with the principles that underlie it.' (Sir Keith Joseph, 23 February 1971.) Its terms of reference were:

> To review the operation of the Abortion Act 1967 and on the basis that the conditions for legal abortion contained in paragraphs (a) and (b) of subsection (1), and in subsections (2), (3) and (4) of Section 1 of the Act remain unaltered, to make recommendations.

The Committee was not to open itself to moral and ethical debates. It could recommend neither the abolition of the law, nor free abortion on demand without restrictions. Its terms of reference permitted it merely to suggest how the law could be efficiently operated.

The Lane Committee sat for three years. It amassed vast quantities of information, heard representations from nearly 200 organizations and published a three volume report in April 1974. Rarely has such a thorough and extensive report been dismissed so easily.

The Report fundamentally supported the 1967 Act, and what recommendations it made, merely required administrative alterations. ALRA found in Lane substance and verification for their arguments for technical modifications, and more extensive sexual and contraceptive education. The anti-abortionists having secured the Enquiry, were disappointed by its recommendations. More importantly they found that some of their arguments had been disproved. Concerned to have a report that would reveal the 'scandals' and 'malpractices' resulting from the Act, and hopefully, recommendations that would restrict abortion, they were perplexed by the conclusions of the Committee:

> we are unanimous in supporting the Act and its provisions. We have no doubt that the gains facilitated by the Act have much outweighed any disadvantages for which it has been criticised. The problems which we have identified in its working, and they are admittedly considerable, are problems for which solutions should be sought by administrative and professional action, and by better education of the public. They are not, we believe, indications that the grounds set out in the Act should be amended in a restrictive way. To do so when the number of unwanted pregnancies is increasing and before comprehensive services are available to all who need them would be to increase the sum of human suffering and ill-health, and probably to drive more women to seek the squalid and dangerous help of the back-street abortionist. [Lane Committee, L605, 1974.]

This conclusion could well have come from ALRA. Sympathetic to the necessity of abortion to 'promote both individual happiness and social stability', tolerant of changing attitudes of women – 'an increasing number of women prefer to follow careers rather than devote themselves exclusively to family life' – Lane was none the less not prepared to support abortion on 'comparatively trivial grounds of inconvenience or embarrassment'.

Although Lane acknowledged that 'there is no measure of total need', it stressed that the rising number of legal abortions was a temporary reaction to the easing of social restraints. Facilities should be provided, but they need not be considered permanent. In time better contraception and education would obviate the need for abortion services.

> A public better educated to a more mature and responsible attitude to sexual behaviour and to contraception will be the most sure guarantee that recourse is made less often to the therapeutic abortion of unwanted pregnancies. [Lane Committee, L609, 1974.]

Meanwhile, abortion can lessen social problems, alleviate distress and suffering. An 'abortion prone' minority is separated from the responsible and rational majority of women. Hence Lane's justification of abortion for the very young:

> A minority of these girls are seriously disturbed and as they develop through adolescence increasingly manifest psychopathic traits. Typically their work record is poor, their personal relationships unstable, and their sense of social responsibility is either markedly underdeveloped or lacking altogether: repeated illegitimate pregnancies, suicidal attempts, venereal infections, delinquency, and abortions may occur. It is in this psychopathic group too that addiction to alcohol and drugs is common, and cruelty to and battering of infants much to be feared. [Lane Committee, L237, 1974.]

Lane blamed many of the abuses and malpractices of the Act on the failure to provide adequate services to meet the demand for abortions.

> The medical and nursing professions had scant time in which to adapt their attitudes and practice to a radically new situation and views tended initially to become polarised for and against the Act. Neither was the NHS in numbers of staff and facilities equipped to meet the heavy demand for increased services. [Lane Committee, L601, 1974.]

The result has been regional discrepancies and inequalities, and women with adequate reasons for abortion within the Act have had to resort to the private sector. Backing the continuation of the private sector, Lane acknowledged the abuses within it but attributed them to a 'small minority of doctors' who for financial gain flouted the provisions of the Act and allowed abortion on request. These abuses could be curtailed and equality realized by bureaucratic and administrative amendments. Radical changes in the terms for abortion, or in facilities were considered unnecessary. In particular, Lane rejected abortion on demand, saying that 'in principle, and in the great majority of instances it is in the woman's own interest that the decision should remain a medical one'. [Lane Committee, L602, 1974.]

Lane and the reformers recognize abuses, excesses and inequalities. Lane furthermore attributed most of the failures to the lack of adequate NHS facilities. Surely the logical step would be free, quick and widely available abortion in the NHS? But to concede abortion on demand would be not only to admit that present social and economic structures are inadequate and can be ameliorated by abortion, but also to collude with what Lane termed the 'unacceptable extremes of individualistic behaviour' which threatened the traditional female role. Licences, controls and inspectorates added to the 1967 Act would in their estimation achieve a fair and equal availability of abortions without permitting abortion on demand.

The Lane Report passed into history, almost without comment. Minor controls like stricter licensing procedures for the private commercial abortion bureaux were implemented. Significantly, no attempt was made to improve and strengthen services inside or outside the NHS. True, the total number of abortions on British residents began to decline slightly after 1973 (110,000 in 1973, 107,000 in 1975), but that did not mean, as Barbara Castle and ALRA took it to mean that the 'peak has now been passed'. Given that the Minister of Health controls the licensing of abortion clinics and that she implemented a gradual tightening of licensing provision during this period, it was absurd for Barbara Castle to pretend that the number of abortions performed reflected a real demand rather than administrative arrangements. It was the lack of facilities, not the lack of demand, which gave rise to the declining figures.

Furthermore, since many of the failures and abuses of the abortion law are, as Lane pointed out, a consequence of the lack of NHS facilities it would seem that the government is unwittingly aiding and abetting the anti-abortionists in discrediting the 1967 Act. It is significant that *NHS* abortions, as a proportion of the total, declined from 65 per cent to an estimated 50 per cent even during the periods of rising total demand.

The necessity for private and commercial bureaux has maintained and strengthened the potential for abuses and exploitation

42

while the incidence of 'abortion on demand', far from being curtailed, has been increased. The 1967 Act provided ammunition for its opponents, and even its supporters; it was inevitable that the abortion debate would be revitalized.

Ironically it was not the anti-abortionists but some of the 1967 Act's supporters who brought the issue back to Parliament. While ALRA were content with the Act and saw the increase in number of abortions as a mere transference from the illegal to the legal sector, the more conservative reformers who considered abortion more strictly as a therapeutic measure designed to alleviate fringe problems, decided that events had overtaken them. Their limited aims had been wildly exceeded.

They considered that 'abortion on demand' had become a reality – and for the very group for whom 'social grounds' could not be pleaded within the Act. They blamed 'psychopathic' doctors who were interpreting the law outside its spirit. They also realized that more facilities would boost the total and lead to more abortion on demand.

For them the real intentions of 1967 could be restored by stopping the loopholes in the Act. New restrictions would outlaw abortion on demand and permit it for the fringe groups only.

That was what prompted the Abortion (Amendment) Bill of 1975, introduced by James White, Labour MP for Glasgow (Pollock). Although labelled by ALRA and some of the press as anti-abortionists, White and Abse, his main supporter in parliament, are justified in claiming that they have been misrepresented. They have consistently denied that they are against abortion as such, they have merely opposed the abuses of the 1967 Act. As one newspaper comment put it:

The Abortion (Amendment) Bill now before the House is, however, a valiant attempt to assuage the sense of outrage felt by the anti-abortionists, while implementing the original intention of the Abortion Act that in particular circumstances abortion would be available to the women in difficulties. It is seeking to wrestle with the major defect of the original Act which is causing most of the present problems, and indeed thwarting the intentions of the legislators to

43

ensure that abortion did not take place for trivial and frivolous reasons. [M.Bateman, *Sunday Times*, 27 April 1975.]

Yet the suspicions of the progressive reformers are easy to understand. For the Amendment's main backers are the anti-abortionists (SPUC); White's motives are clearly inspired by electoral considerations: 'I'd never thought about abortion until the 1970 election'; and furthermore the Amendment could not achieve its ostensible aims.

White's campaign focused on the abuses: the touting, rackets, and liberal interpretation of the Act. Yet denunciation of the abuses was merely a ploy to abolish 'abortion on demand'. They believed that by amending the Act, and annihilating the abuses, the spirit of the 1967 Act could be restored, thus allowing abortion where it will alleviate pain and suffering: 'I would have voted for the original Abortion Bill . . . Until such time as the "New Jerusalem" comes along with no bad housing, no poverty and no alcoholic husbands, I insist that abortion must be available for women with problems.' (James White, introducing the Second Reading.)

The reforming assumptions of 1967 were the backbone of White's stance. Both he and Abse denied that they wanted to scrap the 'social grounds' for abortion. Their indignation arose from the possible 'trivial' and 'frivolous' use of abortion and the rising numbers of abortions in this country.

> We also intend to take care of abortion on demand. There are some 200,000 abortions done in this country every year and we think it is too many. We think people are using abortion instead of birth control. We don't want to make it difficult for the following categories: women with larger families, single women, young girls or women with housing problems. But we certainly don't think a woman should be able to have an abortion just because she wants to. [James White, *Guardian*, 6 February 1975.]

The *central* concern is abortion on demand, and James White admits that arguments about exploitation, touts and rackets are just fuses to the gunpowder:

44

I think that it is necessary to pin-point what the abuse is. The abuse was overcharging but it is not anymore, and it is no good bringing in regulations to stop overcharging when the overcharging has sorted itself out and the abuse is now, if you like, in mass production with undercharging. [Select Committee discussions, 23 June 1975.]

For James White and his allies it is clear that in the end there is only one abuse – 'on demand is the abuse' (Leo Abse) – and it must be stopped.

James White's acceptance of abortion for 'women with social problems' goes hand in hand with Sir Keith Joseph's argument that the 'cycle of deprivation could be broken' if the poorest, most demoralized and deprived sectors of the community could be persuaded to have fewer children. The Amendment was aimed at changing the uneven access to abortion for women of different classes – where the Abortion Act 1967 gave preferential access to the upper middle classes, the Amendment, it was assumed, would give priority to working class women. It was a reformist proposal. It placed abortion in the context of a palliative to social problems and in doing so elicited much parliamentary support. Given the premises of the Amendment Act, it is hardly surprising that White gained support from so many Labour MPs and that Leo Abse, renowned for his part in liberal reforms (homosexuality, contraception and divorce) should be co-sponsor of the Act.

3.
The Abortion Amendment Bill

On 7 February 1975 the Abortion Amendment Bill was given a second reading by 203 votes to 88 and referred to a select committee, where old debates and well-worn themes were revived. At issue in 1966 were ambiguous legislation, criminal (i.e. illegal) abortions and the presence of a large profitable private market which provided abortion on demand for a price. In 1975, the issues were again criminal (in the sense of abuses of) abortion, ambiguous legislation and a private sector allowing abortion on demand. The protagonists had become powerful organizations and movements and the arguments now ranged from the 'right to life' to the 'right to choose'.

The Bill's sponsors formed a strange medley. Teddy Taylor, Tory MP for Glasgow (Cathcart) admitted: 'I am opposed to abortion', and Donald Steward believed 'that it is a grave sin'. On the other hand, James White, although attacked by supporters of abortion and in sections of the media as an anti-abortionist, could truthfully say: 'I take no hard line on abortion . . . I and my fellow sponsors give our word to the House that no tricks are being played. We want to make the 1967 Act work as it was intended to work.' The Bill 'does not seek to limit the existing grounds for abortion'. (James White.)

The core of the argument was whether to permit 'abortion on demand' which had grown up in some of the interstices of the 1967 Act, or not. By attacking the Act for allowing its intentions to be abused, and in particular erasing its liberal social clause White hoped to ensure that abortion on demand would be resisted, while the marginally deprived and demoralized sectors of the population would still have recourse to the abortions which could alleviate their problems.

Ironically the proposed Amendment legislation bore an uncanny resemblance to Lord Silkin's earlier abortion bills and Steel's Medical Termination of Pregnancy Bill 1966. But what was considered too radical in 1966 – and indeed revised into the more cautious 1967 Act – became a platform for White and his allies in 1975.

White's Bill was badly put together. He was, as Madeleine Simms commented: 'badly served by his colleagues who drafted the bill for him. The bill is long, complex and quite clearly destructive in intention.' [M.Simms, 'The progress of the Abortion Amendment Bill', 1975.]

Consideration of the terms reveals that the Bill clearly intended to restrict 'abortion on demand'. It also shows the Bill's recommendations would hardly have alleviated the situation of the marginal cases which were the Bill's ostensible concern. On the contrary, they would have severely limited access to abortions. Inevitably the knitting needles, gin baths, back street abortions and the discreet, élite Harley Street surgeries would have returned. And it would be precisely the marginal, grave and serious cases for whom the Bill was intended who would be least successful in obtaining legal abortions.

The Clauses of the Abortion Amendment Bill

1. The 1967 Act permitted abortion with the consent of two medical practitioners. The new Bill would require that the two doctors must have been practising for five years and that they be not employed in the same practice.

This clause was a clear attack on those 'psychopathic doctors' who have interpreted the 1967 Act liberally. Psychopathy, it seems, is contagious and is a product of youth. Or is it assumed that liberalism is mere youthful naivety? Furthermore, the clause questions the adequacy, training and professional competence of the medical profession. If, after training, doctors are considered incompetent to make decisions on the relatively minor medical issue of abortion, what confidence can the public bestow upon them for any other form of treatment?

If the clause's intention was to curb the private sector, its framers had a very naive view of profit-making organizations. Only 16 per cent of doctors are under thirty. The majority of doctors in private practice have more than five years' experience, and two doctors determined to make money are not likely to find it difficult to conspire from two different practices – one might assume that it would be a standard procedure in any illegal activity!

However the five year practice rule could prevent some women from getting treatment from their local GPs. It is also clear that obtaining the consent of a second doctor would *delay* abortion and make it less safe since it is important for abortions to occur early in pregnancy. Delays and restrictions, particularly within the NHS, would force women to seek treatment in the private sector, or to support an unwanted child.

Within the private sector, the Amendment required there to be a medical practitioner of consultant status. The many attempts to include a consultant clause in the Abortion Act had always met opposition, not least from the medical profession. This part of the clause constituted a new attack on the medical profession and was meant to restrict the number of abortions. That women forced into the private sector, because of deficiencies in the NHS, should encounter more severe restrictions in the private sector is ridiculous. Free and widely available abortion in the NHS would erase the abuses of the private sector.

2. The opponents of abortion on demand believe that the fundamental problem in the Act is the 'loophole' clause. This allows abortion where it is thought that continuation of pregnancy would risk injuring the woman's physical and mental health more than the termination. It is this clause condemned by Leo Abse for

allowing 'pernicious statistical argument', that permits abortion on demand.

Undoubtedly the clause has allowed a liberal interpretation that has, to quote the Lane report, 'relieved a vast amount of suffering' amongst women. Unfortunately it has also ensured that abortion remains a medical issue – that abortions are carried out for therapeutic and medical reasons. It denies the modest but crucial demand of women for control of their own bodies.

> By the time she comes to see me, a woman has usually worked out why she wants an abortion. I just need to see that she has some knowledge of the alternatives. . . . But I do think it is humiliating and degrading for a woman to have to come in here and exaggerate her distress, or convince me that she wants an abortion.
> What is silly is the pretence being kept up that we are doing therapeutic abortion for medical reasons. It would be better if we would be honest and then we'd cease to be in the position of playing God. In practice if I'm faced with a girl wanting an abortion why do I have to test how distressed she is? All I get is a charade played out for me. [Peter Diggory, *Guardian*, 6 February 1975.]

Sheila Young in a study of doctors' attitudes to abortion comments on the doctor's role in decision-making:

> The doctor not only takes over the woman's decision; he also puts that decision within a framework of conventional morality – inextricably intermingled with science and with his professional status – a morality that takes as its base-line the nuclear family and sees deviations from this model as situations which it is his province to correct. He does not see it as part of his role critically to examine or to correct the model. [S.Young, *Radical Science Journal*, no.2/3, 1975, p.58.]

Analysing liberal doctors' attitudes to abortion, Sheila Young notes their expressions of 'paternalism and protectionism for the "hegemony" of the family as the correct and healthy living unit'. The 1967 Act allows for *medical* discretion, it denies *women* rights over their own bodies, and so confirms the traditional idea of the family. Sheila Young concludes by showing how this works out in practice:

49

A strange sort of game is being played out. On the whole the doctor will not refuse an abortion provided the patient asks for it rather than demands it. The doctor has to see the patient as contrite – as desirous of maintaining the present forms of social organisation rather than of disrupting them. This deviant behaviour is subsumed within present structures. The stray sheep is returned to the fold. [Sheila Young, *Radical Science Journal*, no.2/3, 1975, p.64.]

The game, however, would be limited if the Amendment's supporters have their way. Medical discretion would be curbed. The new Bill would change grounds (a), (b) and (c) by substituting for 'greater than' the concepts 'grave risk' and 'serious injury'. Lord Silkin's Bill and Steel's initial draft Medical Termination of Pregnancy Bill 1966 had both included the wording 'grave and serious', words that in 1967 were considered both medically restrictive and legally ambiguous. As David Steel reminded James White, these words were dropped in 1967 after advice from the BMA and RCOG who saw such phrasing as:

capable of causing considerable difficulties in practice and may mean that terminations carried out on certain medical indications which are accepted under current medical practice would become questionable in future. [ALRA/A Woman's Right to Choose Campaign, *Memorandum to Select Committee on the Abortion Amendment Bill*, 1975, p.7.]

Legal ambiguities contributed to the reform of abortion legislation: the Amendment would have renewed uncertainty. 'Grave and serious' would have had no meaning in law until there had been a series of test cases which might take as long as ten years. If the history of abortion has revealed anything it is that where definitions are ambiguous, one thing we can be certain of is that they will have to be revised.

This is the most restrictive clause in the Amendment Bill. Although theoretically doctors would still be able to take into account the environment of the women or their existing families, the 'grounds' would be stricter and less women would get abortions. Moreover, given the medical profession's hostility to such vague phrases, one can hazard a guess that it would adopt a cautious stance towards abortion.

This was true before 1967. Had the Amendment Bill become law, *extreme* caution would have prevailed. The 1967 Act made clinical judgements final, the White Bill breached the medical defence. Clause 11 recommended that the onus to prove the risk of serious injury rested with the doctor. Further, the Bill breached the tradition that until proved guilty a person is innocent in law. As ALRA/A Woman's Right to Choose noted:

> Mr White's Bill puts doctors and other professional workers into a category analagous with persons found carrying offensive weapons and persons carrying tools apparently for use in 'breaking and entering', the two most notable exceptions to this principle of British justice. [ALRA/A Woman's Right to Choose Campaign, *Memorandum to Select Committee on the Abortion Amendment Bill*, 1975, p.15.]

The Amendment's recommendations for 'grave and serious' were intended mainly to end abortion on demand. Both legally and morally the concept of 'greater risk' has been seen to hold more weight. As Joyce Butler, Labour MP for Wood Green, commented in the Select Committee: 'What I do not understand is how it can be considered unlawful for a woman to take the lesser rather than the greater risk?'

And the World Health Organization, concerned to ensure the 'harmonious relations and security of all peoples', comments:

> The choice currently being offered lies between legalising first trimester abortion on request, or a list of indications for abortion. Nonetheless, the principle in the British Abortion Act 1967 that abortion should be legal if 'the continuance of the pregnancy would involve risk . . . of injury to the physical or mental health of the pregnant woman . . . greater than if the pregnancy were terminated' should be endorsed. [International Planned Parenthood Federation, Europe Region, 1973, p.19.]

To uphold the 1967 Act, is to deny women the *right* to abortion because it makes abortion a *medical* decision. To further curtail the existing grounds for abortion by inserting the words 'grave and serious' is to severely restrict the scope and availability of abortions. It is not a token limitation; as Madeleine Simms put it when commenting on the 1967 Act, the 'whole concept of "grounds" for legal abortion is a fiction'. [M.Simms, 'The Abortion Act after three years', 1971, pp.269-286.] For although the rich could always go back to Harley Street, as they did before 1967, the poor, unable to express the gravity of their case, would be forced to accept the unwanted child.

3. The Amendment Bill suggested reducing the time factor in abortions. At present abortions are legal within 28 weeks of pregnancy. The majority occur within 12 weeks of pregnancy (80 per cent in 1973) while late abortions (after 20 weeks) account for less than 1 per cent of the total.

The White Amendment sought to curtail abortions after 20 weeks, permitting them up to 24 weeks only where resuscitation equipment was available and where strong evidence existed that the foetus was seriously damaged physically or mentally. After 12 weeks, and increasingly as one reaches the later stages of pregnancy, abortion becomes a slightly more 'dangerous' operation. However, late terminations are frequently the product of inadequate facilities, delays in referral and treatment or a consequence of the biased and idiosyncratic decisions of the medical profession.

Late terminations are more frequent in the NHS than in the private sector. Given the demand for specialized equipment and a consultant, and given the current cutback in public expenditure, the Amendment would only increase delays and therefore the number of terminations. Private clinics would however be less restricted. Late terminations would remain expensive and profits would provide the equipment.

Although the proportion of abortions occurring after 17 weeks is declining, and abortions occurring in the first three months are slowly increasing, the likelihood of very early abortions remains minimal. Pregnancy tests are frequently unreliable until two weeks after a period is overdue, and restrictions on resources and research seem to hamper the availability of immediate, reliable procedures for determining pregnancy. Recent reports in *Spare Rib* [no.41, p.20] of the 'conception' test, which can determine pregnancy ten days after conception reveal that although available in the commercial sector, its use as a routine service is unlikely. At present, it is used in research projects at a London hospital. Resources are limited to only one technician for one day a week.

Technology has not it seems brought immediate and reliable pregnancy tests. On the other hand sophisticated medical techniques have made the survival of a foetus at an earlier stage possible. Children born between the 24th and 28th week of pregnancy have occasionally survived. Legal and medical authorities throughout the world are reviewing the upper limits of abortion in this light. So long as foetus viability is equated with the sanctity of life, medical advances threaten to reduce the rights of women to control their own fertility. If adequate abortion facilities were available early termination would counteract this trend. But the Amendment would simultaneously *reduce* facilities and the *upper limit* for abortion. This would result in an even greater proportion of women being ineligible than would occur if the 24 week limit were introduced with the present facilities.

It is frequently the woman who has failed to obtain *early* termination who most needs an abortion. To seek one later is a product of extreme desperation. Ironically, this would be more likely amongst those marginal cases which the reformers claim to want to help. Women already overburdened by a large family or the 14 year old girl too naive and frightened to recognize her condition are most likely to seek late abortions. Even the Lane Committee using extremely restricted categories admitted:

> There is a number, albeit small, of cases of women presenting for abortion between the twentieth and twenty-fourth weeks of pregnancy, who nevertheless have compelling grounds for termination and should not be precluded from obtaining it. These include women who develop or manifest a serious medical or obstetric condition and a few with a serious mental condition. [Lane Committee, L279, 1974.]

Nor would the ban on late abortions curb excesses in the private sector. Late terminations would command the highest fees and be open to the greatest degree of exploitation.

4. James White's prime concern to curtail abortion on demand was apparent in the Bill's restrictions on referral and advisory agencies. The Amendment made illegal any fee or reward for referring women to agencies, doctors or clinics. This would have eliminated the taxi-touts and agencies who recommend doctors and clinics for a fee. However the Bill then set further restrictions that would have made it extremely difficult for anyone other than medical practitioners or persons approved by the Secretary of State to obtain or give *any* advice or information regarding abortion. Existing general advice agencies such as Release or Citizens Advice Bureaux would, unless approved by the state, have been acting illegally in giving any information on abortion. But even *that* was not sufficient for the Bill made it a statutory requirement that all people giving advice inform women of the alternatives to abortion. Furthermore, for anyone breaking the law, the Bill provided draconic penalties. As ALRA comments:

> Having put every remunerated person who might be asked or be expected to advise or give information on obtaining abortion into a straitjacket, this final sub-section bolts and bars the door. *Anyone* who contravenes or fails to comply with *any* of the provisions of Clause 5 shall be guilty of an offence and, according to Clause 11, the onus of proof shall rest on the accused person. It would be hard to imagine a greater restriction of the right to knowledge. [ALRA/A Woman's Right to Choose Campaign, *Memorandum to Select Committee on the Abortion Amendment Bill*, 1975, p.21.]

The Amendment would not merely have restricted the medical grounds for abortion, but it would have placed abortion clearly in the realm of the clandestine, the immoral, and the taboo. Another section of the proposed measures would have made it illegal to publish 'the identity, or any information or particulars calculated to lead to the identification' of any woman seeking advice or obtaining an abortion. Abortion would no longer be a medical issue, but a tainted subject liable to deprave and corrupt. Women would not even be permitted to write about their abortion experiences, censorship would exist, the freedom of the press would be curtailed.

Although White's purpose seems to have been to bury information and knowledge on abortion and so clean up the 'abortion climate', the effect of such measures would confound his reforming concerns. For it would be the marginal sectors, the naive, the over-burdened and less well educated women who would suffer. Lack of time, knowledge and finance have always meant that it is harder for some women than for others to get abortions; limiting information would make this situation more unequal. Repressive measures would only delay abortions, making them less safe, and undoubtedly the illegal and quasi-legal entrepreneurs would be back in business. Leo Abse commenting on the Amendment said it aimed 'to close the controversy' once and for all. Certainly the recommended legislation on information and advice would make 'controversy' virtually impossible.

5. Under the present abortion legislation, parental consent is necessary before an abortion can be carried out on a girl under sixteen. This restriction would have been further emphasized by the Amendment. It would have demanded that parents be present when any advice on abortion was given to a girl under sixteen. This additional measure reflects the reformers' ideological concern with the nuclear family. They argue that abortion for a young girl is not a decision that is hers alone. Children are synonymous with the family and decisions about them must therefore be made by the family. These young girls are seen as naive and inadequate, incapable of making a decision for themselves. For James White they are 'wee lassies' who have been pressurized into bed by 'bandits' (sic) and rightly owed the operation, but parents should be party to all discussions and decisions.

6. James White used 'abuses' as the justification for restrictions. They served as a front behind which the wider reformist

concerns of the reformers could be masked, whilst mass support for their Bill was being gathered. This was particularly true of the Amendment's restriction on abortions for foreign women. It was a powerful issue. The notion that London was becoming the 'abortion capital' of the world served to stir up moral indignation and rally support for restrictions. Singling out foreign women focused attention on the abuses and diverted the public eye from the more extensive repressive intentions of the Act. In fact there had been a gradual decline in the number of foreign women seeking abortions in the previous four years. As other countries liberalized their abortion legislation, the need for women to come to England lessened. Had White's Bill become law the traffic in abortion might well have reversed as British women unable to seek attention at home sought abortions abroad.

The Intended Effect

Medical hierarchy and ideologies, together with the financial and bureaucratic limitations of the NHS, have restricted the number and distribution of abortion facilities in the country. Chronic lack of finance in the Health Service, shortage of staff and pressure on facilities have promoted continuing growth of private and charitable abortion agencies. The result has been a gradual decrease in the proportion of NHS abortions and a rise in private abortions.

We have shown that the rise in private abortions provided fuel for an attack on the private sector. The reformers used the abuses in the private sector to press for new legislation. They ignored the economic advantages of abortion. However, their prime concern is ideological. They aim to permit abortion only where it will alleviate social problems and strengthen the nuclear family. They have made no mention of the abuses in the health service, the unequal and slow access to abortions, the very reasons for which a private/charitable sector had developed.

Despite claims that they merely wished to stop abuses and not to limit the existing grounds for abortion, the Bill's sponsors clearly expected a reduction in legal abortions. Mr Andrew Bowden, a co-sponsor of the Bill, estimated that the number would fall to about 60-70,000 legal abortions if the Bill became law. If this estimate is based on the 54,000 abortions on foreign women in 1974, none of which would then be permissible, there would be a reduction of 15,000 abortions on residents. White and his supporters claimed that this estimated cut of 15,000 would occur in the abortion on demand sector. Abortion legislation would work as intended, only the 'deprived', the 'sick' and the 'inadequate' would obtain treatment.

We have shown how false this is. Some women, with access to the relatively simple Karman cannula vacuum abortion technique would try do-it-yourself abortions; others would once again turn to the back street abortionist. Women would be forced to engage in risks. Exploitation, ill-health and death would be almost inevitable. The private sector would grow, illegal abortion would flourish, and abuses prosper. The deprived marginal sectors, the 'sick', 'inadequate' and 'overburdened' would be forced to accept the unwanted child. That the 'bells have begun to toll for the avaricious' (Leo Abse) is questionable, but the bells have certainly begun to toll for women.

The Select Committee

The Select Committee was appointed in February 1975. Its task: to consider the Amendment Bill, receive written or oral evidence on abortion, and make recommendations. It was a biased Committee: its 27 per cent of women represent the 52 per cent of women in the country; its 20 per cent of Roman Catholics represent the 14 per cent of Catholics in the country.

However, the prospects of immediate changes by the Committee were weakened when the medical profession gave support to the 1967 Act: 'We would not wish the wording of the Act, which lays down the criteria, to be altered. We prefer the balanced judgement that we are used to making in other parts of our medical practice.' (A.Dickens, BMA.) It was further weakened by the extremes to which the anti-abortionists went in presenting their case, in particular the heavy publicity surrounding the notorious book *Babies for Burning* and the fact that the tapes on which it was allegedly based to a great extent were never forthcoming. But the Committee's intentions remained: not so much to check the abuses, but as Leo Abse said, 'the purpose of this is that it is directed against those back-sliders who may not be performing therapeutic abortion, but abortion on demand.'

A three-sided confrontation occurred within Parliament and the Select Committee. James White and the conservative reformers wanted legislative change in order to curb 'abortion on demand'. They were backed by the anti-abortionists who saw in White the possibility of a strategic advance in the battle towards total abolition of abortion. The progressive reformers denied that abortion on demand was occurring and supported the 1967 Act. All sides agreed that there were abuses; for the supporters of the 1967 Act the abuses derived from there being unequal and insufficient facilities. For the conservative reformers and their anti-abortionist backers the abuses ranged from touting to abortion per se. The progressive reformers demanded administrative change whilst White and his supporters wanted legislative change. The Amendment Bill and Select Committee have become a focus for the opposing sides in the debate. Influenced by the women's movement ALRA emerged from its semi-retirement rejuvenated by younger and more radical supporters. It started a new campaign, 'A Woman's Right To Choose', while remaining mainly a pressure and information group.

As women throughout the country became more aware of the Amendment and alarmed at its implications a new group emerged – the National Abortion Campaign (NAC). Based on the woman's movement, with groups throughout the country NAC fought alongside ALRA for a woman's right to choose and against the Amendment. Abortion was no longer the concern of an élite pressure group but the focus of a mass movement.

The anti-abortionists, spear-headed by SPUC, were not idle

58

either. Highly organized, based on church bodies, it too developed a mass movement.

Both sides rallied thousands of people. Abortion became an emotional issue with support comparable to the anti-Vietnam war movement or the Campaign for Nuclear Disarmament.

Throughout the summer of 1975 the Select Committee continued to gather evidence, argue, compromise and bargain. On 20 July that year it issued an interim report containing a set of recommendations for administrative regulation, the first step to restrictive and repressive legislation, and, on 21 October 1975, Barbara Castle, Minister of Health told the House of Commons that 'the Government accept in principle all the Select Committee's recommendations.'

She went on:

> I should like to see a more uniform and better coverage of provision in the NHS which is one of the Lane Committee's recommendations, because this would reduce dependence on the private sector which has been the source of abuse.

Castle said nothing about improving NHS facilities. On the contrary, she produced recommendations that will increasingly hamper and delay abortions both in the private and public sectors:

1. A scale of fees to be introduced in the private sector. Reducing the fees will no doubt allow the NHS to lean more heavily on the private sector. But despite some moves by the present government to eliminate private medicine, in the area of abortion they still seem to condone and encourage it.

2. No hospital to carry out abortions after 20 weeks without resuscitation equipment. The extreme and severe instances where abortion is most vital, to be curbed. Since the Select Committee agreed that no foetus under 24 weeks can survive, the restriction to 20 weeks can only be seen as a means to limit the number of abortions.

3. Records of foreign women having abortions to be kept. The Department to prevent a majority of foreign women being treated in any one clinic 'if necessary'.

4. The government to publish a list of approved referral agencies. Clinics taking patients from unapproved agencies to lose their licences; and circulars to be published to ensure adequate counselling before and after an abortion decision. This measure's power to restrict advice, information and access to abortions is limitless but it is not yet known just which agencies, groups, or charities are to gain Department approval.

5. Bureaucratic procedures to be tightened up. Certification and notification forms to be numbered consecutively and sent by registered post to the Department. As Madeleine Simms pointed out, to make this proposal in the same week as severe cut-backs in the NHS were announced was absurd. But not altogether absurd for however costly and time-consuming, it would also provide a close control on the precise numbers and reasons for pregnancy termination.

Implementing these measures may curtail some of the existing abuses, but cumbersome procedures and restrictions on information and advice will certainly reduce the number of abortions. Restrictive measures are *already* operating, and the debate has not yet closed.

The Future

The Abortion Amendment Bill fell at the end of the parliamentary session, along with the Select Committee. All that resulted directly were the measures announced by Barbara Castle to restrict existing abortion legislation and eliminate existing abuses. However, in January 1976, the House decided to reconvene the Select Committee on a free vote. More MPs voted than ever before on abortion. 113 Labour MPs voted in favour – a larger number than voted for the James White Amendment. It indicated a pronounced swing against 'abortion on demand' despite all NAC's efforts.

Within a week of the reconvening the six committee members who hold progressive views on abortion resigned en bloc protesting that the Committee was patently biased against the 1967 Act. However, the Select Committee remained in being with its bias unchanged. NAC and ALRA were the first witnesses to be called to give oral evidence before it. NAC refused and made itself liable for breach of parliamentary privilege. At the same time, together with a number of pro-abortion organizations, NAC formed a committee to oppose collaboration with the Select Committee.

When the Select Committee finally makes its recommendations it will be up to the government or any private member to propose legislation. In the present political climate it would seem that women's abortion rights – limited as they are – will *increasingly* come under attack despite the mass mobilization in their defence. At the same time, the debate is becoming increasingly polarized, with NAC clearly taking up an abortion on demand stance which separates it from the entire spectrum of parliamentary opinion *including* the progressive reformers. Whilst parliament swings against the 1967 Act as being too permissive, NAC is increasingly critical of its restrictions.

The expenditure cuts inflicted on the NHS underline the threat to existing abortion facilities. It is an area where economies can easily be made. Indeed some people consider the decline in the number of abortions to be due as much to the cut-backs as to medical caution in the face of the uproar on the abortion issue.

If financial restraint were the only consideration, more weight would be given to day-care clinics, the most effective and straightforward abortion service. Yet, although attention is turning to their establishment, constraints and caution are the watchword. Barbara Castle issued a circular encouraging regional hospital boards to study and establish day-care facilities, but circulars are notorious for their ineffectiveness. Whether clinics become established will be a matter of discretion for the regional hospital boards and community health authorities. Personal attitudes and values, available facilities and resources will decide the issue. We can assume that unless a statutory obligation is laid on regional health boards to establish day-care services, clinics will be few and far between.

Schemes are also afoot to give permission to charitable

agencies to establish day clinics. Once more greater stress is laid on the need for stringent controls, than on the need for facilities.

The *Guardian* (3 January 1976) reported that charitable agencies may be required to take patients referred by GPs from a limited catchment area, and to refer them back to the care of a local GP – measures that are more stringent than those for a patient discharged after an over-night stay. It also reported that the Department of Health would require clinics to keep an empty bed available for each patient in case an over-night stay was needed.

It is absurd to bring in a potentially cheap, safe, quick and effective method of abortion and then defeat its purpose by constraints that will limit access to it and maintain the present costs. The motives can only be the desire to limit access to, and control the total number of, abortions.

While other countries introduce liberal abortion legislation, and quick, safe and effective abortion services, Britain seems to be stepping backwards. James White and his colleagues may have achieved some gains in the attempt to curtail abortion on demand, but they have confounded their alleged concern for abortion as a palliative to existing social problems. None of the proposed measures, nor the already implemented recommendations, will ensure that abortion is available for the women with social problems. Every restriction favours the wealthy and knowledgeable and deprives the working class women who depend on the NHS.

Only abortion on demand, widely available and free under the NHS can achieve the reformers' declared ends.

4.
The Magic Figure

Estimates of the number of illegal abortions before 1967 range from 15,000 to 100,000 per year. The importance of these figures to the debate centres on the size of the problem which the 1967 Act was brought in to ameliorate, the justification of the Act itself, and the efficacy of the Act in eliminating illegal abortions once implementation was on the way.

Anti-abortionists deny that there were ever many illegal abortions, and suggest that the Act has had little impact on their number. Pro-abortionists, on the other hand, insist that the pre-1967 figure was high and that the effect of the Act was merely to legalize existing practices. There are five basic methods of estimating the number of illegal abortions.

1. Hospital emergency admissions

In the 1960s between 70-80,000 women every year were received into hospitals as emergency abortion cases with complications arising from pregnancy. About 20 per cent of all conceptions end in spontaneous abortion (i.e. miscarriages) so some proportion of these feature in the emergency admissions.

To arrive at the number of illegal abortions from the emergency admissions requires the following calculations. First, an estimate of the number that are the result of interference, i.e. nonspontaneous. Second, an estimate of the ratio of illegal abortions which required hospital admission to those which were comparatively safe.

The usual procedure is to take a sample of hospitals and

enquire of the gynaecologists what proportion of abortions were the result of interference, apply this figure to all admissions, and multiply the result by an estimate of the proportion of safe illegal abortions.

A more sophisticated approach relies on the proportion of septic abortions in the total. [G.B.Goodhart, 1973, pp.207-218.] But this does not avoid the general criticisms that can be made of the method.

First, the sample of hospitals would have to be typical for the country as a whole. All women admitted would have to be presumed as coming from the hospital area concerned; and the variation in hospitals' 'reputations' as being 'liberal' in the abortion field would have to be discounted.

Secondly, there is no logical reason why a particular proportion of 'safe' to 'complicated' illegal abortions should be fixed (it is usually considered to be a ratio of 3 : 1). Furthermore, improvements in the antibiotics used in illegal abortions would render even this figure unreliable as a fixed figure over time; and there is no reason to assume that illegal abortion techniques do not vary widely across the country. In the former instance, it is important to note that there has been a progressive reduction of emergency hospital admissions for women. All in all, this approach is too speculative to be credible except as a back-up figure.

2. Police figures

Police statistics consist of two sorts : illegal abortions known to the police and the number of persons found guilty of illegal abortions. The statistics on crimes where both parties are consenting (e.g. abortion, prostitution, drugs) are notoriously under-reported and unreliable. Few criminologists would accept them as showing anything but changes in police activity in the particular area concerned. They contribute nothing to the debate on the efficacy of the 1967 Act either in their use by pro-abortionists (e.g. M.Simms, 1970) or by those sceptical of the Act (e.g. J.M.Finnis, 1971).

64

3. National opinion polls

The most frequently cited national opinion poll is that commissioned by ALRA in July 1966. This indicated an annual average of 31,000 abortions per year between 1946 and 1965. The figure is based on a respondent rate of 60 per cent. Given the highly personal nature of the questions asked, the illegality of the procedure and the fact that postal questionnaires are formal, it can be assumed that quite a lot of the 40 per cent who did not reply were afraid to admit they had had an abortion. And of those who replied how many lied? Even in communities where abortion is legal, women will admit to only 50 per cent of the abortions known to have been performed. [W.H.James, 1971, pp.327-338.] So all we can do is take the evidence as a *low* figure.

Further the survey's estimate of 85,000 attempted abortions annually would also be an under-estimate.

4. Effects on birth rate

The stumbling blocks in any calculation based on the effect of abortion on the birth rate are : estimating coital frequency, the changing intentions of couples about family size, and the use of contraceptives. Coital frequency is of minor importance : it is not how often you do it, but the intention that matters. Intention is crucial and of more importance than contraceptive use. In the 1930s, for example, contraception was inefficient, but the birth rate slumped. Even if intentions are quantified, there is a further problem in estimating illegal abortions from data on live births and legal abortions.

The most sophisticated attempt to assess them come from G.B.Goodhart. But he assumes that the pre-1968 illegal abortion rate was constant, and proceeds to demonstrate that the figure must have been much lower than is usually assumed because the legal abortion rate after the Act does not approach anywhere near the size necessary to represent a smooth transfer from the posited illegal rate to the known legal rate. He writes :

c

[this] implies that the criminal abortion rate before 1968 was constant. There is no positive reason for believing this to have been so, and one might have expected increasing knowledge and availability of contraceptives to have reduced the number of unwanted pregnancies, and hence the demand for abortion. But results in this respect seem to have been below expectation, and a recent report on university students in Aberdeen, for example, shows that even highly educated young women in an environment with a well-deserved reputation for progressive sexual attitudes are only too ready to take risks without contraceptive protection. And if, as is widely believed, permissiveness in sexual behaviour has been on the increase, this will raise the number at risk, to balance any reduction due to contraception. But so far as their effect upon criminal abortion is concerned, both these factors will have been proportional to total demand, and since they will have tended to cancel out, there is no particular reason to suppose that illegal abortion was either increasing or decreasing over the years before 1968. [G.B.Goodhart, 1973, p.228.]

We see no reason, whatsoever, to assume that such a cancelling out took place nor is the citing of a study of women students in Aberdeen the sort of material on which to base an elaborate statistical analysis.

5. Illegitimacy rate

The number of illegitimate births rose from 42,707 in 1960 to 66,249 in 1965 in step with the rise in the total number of births. After 1964 the latter began to fall though illegitimacy continued to rise at a somewhat reduced rate to peak at 69,928 in 1967.

The decline in the birth rate was not due to social factors (e.g. changes in the age structure of the population) and is often attributed to the increased use of contraceptives and changes in parental aspirations. If this is the case the illegitimacy rate did not respond as strongly to these factors.

After 1968, however, illegitimacy declined slightly to 67,041 in 1969 and 64,744 in 1970. It is therefore presumed that this represents the impact of the 1967 Act as without the increase in legal abortions, illegitimacy would have gone on rising.

The reformers argue that this surprisingly small decrease occurred because of a simple transference from the illegal to the legal sector – for if all abortions were to have increased, the fall in the illegitimacy rate would have been far greater. This sustains their confidence in their estimate of the illegal abortion figure prior to 1967.

But, just as in the case of deducing a figure from the number of live births, changes in both parental intentions and contraceptive use are unknown. There is no reason, for instance, why unmarried people should not have used contraceptives on a larger scale than married couples. Nor is there any way of knowing if increases in sexual freedom have not put a larger number of unmarried women at risk. Both these factors make accurate calculations either backwards, in terms of the pre-1967 illegal abortion rate, or forwards, in terms of the effect of the Act, extremely difficult.

Both the reformers and their opponents rest their case on the extent of illegal abortion prior to 1967. The former impute a high figure and judge the effect of the Act as a mere transference of abortions from the illegal to the legal sector, and not as an encouragement of abortion. Their opponents argue that the figure was low and that the Act has actively encouraged abortion instead of contraception.

All the estimates are suspect. We also believe the statistics to be irrelevant. Whether there were 15,000 or 100,000 illegal abortions prior to the Act – either figure is lamentable. The problem is to remove illegal abortion as a practice in our society and to create facilities where abortion is a viable alternative for women who wish to terminate pregnancy. If this creates a situation where legal abortions far surpass the number of abortions in the past it would be a clear indication that society is not providing the circumstances for women to give birth. But it would also be an achievement in that it would represent a clear and necessary exercise of a woman's right to control her own fertility in a society as lacking in facilities as our own. Talk of transference is merely a reflection of the reformers' concern to change without altering society's foundations. Talk of abortion consciousness is a time-honoured conservative ploy to suggest that radical demands have already been achieved.

Throughout the debate on abortion one figure occurs with astonishing regularity – 100,000 illegal abortions prior to 1967. Based on two studies of hospital admissions this number was taken up by ALRA with such success that they could claim, 'during parliamentary debates on the Abortion Act, the Home Secretary used this as his base-line figure'. [M.Simms, 'The Abortion Act after three years', 1971, p.271.]

Such a constant figure is suspect. It presumes that the demand for abortion is somehow static, that it does not vary with changes in the position of women, changes in contraceptive usage, and of the actual availability of abortion facilities. When used to judge the success of the 1967 Act it results in surprising pronouncements:

> Abortions in England and Wales decreased significantly in 1974. The initial rapid rise started to level out three years ago and it appears the peak has now been passed. [British Pregnancy Advisory Service, *Abortion Today*, no.1, p.1.]

> As the abortion statistics mounted, they showed that for all its local limitations the Abortion Act had produced a major change in medical practice within the National Health Service. There was, however, no evidence to show that the total number of abortions had increased. On grounds of common sense it seems likely that many women who, before the Act, would have been deterred by the old law, now ask their GPs for abortion. [K.Hindell and M.Simms, 1971, p.218.]

It was almost as if the reformers believed that once the magic figure had been achieved they could rest content. Furthermore, it was as if the government might be judging 100,000 as the palatable limit above which any increase would indicate licence. For statistics, however unreliable, can take on a reality of their own when they are used to determine what facilities should be made available. And to complete the mystification, these statistics which result from the use of available facilities may be cited publicly to

68

show that demand had indeed peaked thus justifying no further extension of resources.

Let us examine the results of the 1967 Act, as shown in Table 1 on page 70.

The following conclusions may be drawn from the table:

1. Total abortions. The total number of abortions has declined since 1973, an estimated reduction of 20,000 by the end of 1975, the vast proportion being made up of foreign women. The fall is a product of the liberalization of abortion laws abroad, particularly in France, but is coupled with increased restrictions on private clinics here. This was undoubtedly the result of pressure on the government and is the most pronounced example of how abortion rates relate to available facilities.

2. Resident abortions. Here we see the phenomenon of peaking and the magic figure. The number of abortions rose rapidly to 108,000 in 1972, peaked at 110,000 in 1973 and has since gradually declined to an estimated 108,000 in 1975. These figures are so close to the estimated number of illegal abortions prior to 1967 as to suggest either that such calculations had an extraordinarily high degree of precision or that there is a magic figure governing the politically permissible level of abortion. We have shown earlier in this chapter that the notion of a static demand for abortion has very little analytical credibility.

Our conclusion, therefore, must be that the figures are largely a function of political decisions and existing medical facilities.

3. National Health Service abortions. From 1972 the number of resident abortions stabilized, and the total figure divided fairly evenly between the private and the public sector. Since statistics do not normally make such convenient breaks spontaneously, one might hazard a guess that an element of public policy was involved. Here we see an extraordinary irony, a Labour Party supposedly committed to a National Health Service condones the existence of a mass surgical operation with a unique proportion of cases in the private sector, and a Labour government pledged

	Total Abortions	Resident Abortions	NHS Abortions (Residents)	Private Abortions (Residents)	% NHS Abortions on Residents Births	Live Births	Live Births Plus Number of Resident Abortions in Previous Year Residents	Abortion Rate per 100 Live Births on Residents
1968	35,000	33,000	21,000	12,000	65	819,000	–	4.0
1969	55,000	50,000	34,000	16,000	67	798,000	831,000	6.3
1970	87,000	76,000	47,000	29,000	62	784,000	834,000	9.7
1971	127,000	95,000	54,000	41,000	57	783,000	859,000	12.1
1972	157,000	108,000	57,000	52,000	52	725,000	820,000	14.9
1973	166,000	110,000	55,000	55,000	50	676,000	784,000	16.3
1974	163,000	109,000	56,000	54,000	51	641,000	750,000	17.0
1975	141,000	107,000	52,000	55,000	49	602,000	711,000	17.6

Table 1. Abortions in England and Wales on Residents by Health Sector and Number of Live Births

to phase out private beds in hospitals actively encourages the maintenance of the private sector in abortions.

As the proportion of National Health Service abortions declines, the reformers' aims in the abortion field are further stymied, because the marginal groups whom they wanted to help are more likely to seek abortions in the public sector, whereas the groups of women whom they would deem less eligible for abortion are more likely to use the private sector.

4. Live births. Live births have declined since 1964 (876,000). If we add the live birth rate to the abortion rate we find that, even allowing for the increase in the number of abortions, the figures have shown a consistent decline. This would indicate that changing aspirations for parenthood and changes in contraceptive use are playing significant roles in reducing the birth rate. It might be conjectured that such a tendency would reduce the number of abortions in the long run.

5. Abortion rate per 100 live births. Since 1968 the number of abortions per 100 live births has increased dramatically. Presumably for the first few years after the Act illegal abortions considerably distorted this figure but the trend continues even after the stabilization of the abortion statistics in 1972. In 1974 one viable foetus in seven was aborted, and in 1975 estimates indicate that the ratio was one in six. Though the parental aspirations and contraceptive use may cut the total number of conceptions the proportion of viable foetuses chosen to be aborted is likely to increase, which makes for a constantly expanding demand for abortion even though facilities remain constant or slightly decline. This should destroy any notion of stabilization in the abortion rate. We can only guess what the rate might be if facilities expanded in a more realistic fashion. Some light may come from looking at the following table of abortion rates per 100 live births in different countries:

Table 2. International Comparison of Abortion Rates per Number of Women and Live Births, 1971

	Number	Rate per 1,000 women age 15-44	Abortion rate per 100 live births
England and Wales	95,000	10.1	12.6
Sweden	19,000	12.2	17.1
Norway	10,000	13.9	18.6
Czechoslovakia	97,000	31.4	39.8
Bulgaria	131,000	69.7	98.5
Hungary	187,000	81.3	122.8
Poland	135,000	17.7	23.6
Japan	740,000	28.2	37.0
New York City	76,000	44.1	62.2

It is generally considered that the abortion rates in Poland and Japan should be double what they appear to be.

It is often argued that the high abortion rate in countries with permissive abortion legislation can be attributed to a lack of contraceptives coupled with a lack of incentive to use them even where they are available. But it is more complicated than this:

Even in countries where pills and IUDs are available, accepted and increasingly used (Sweden and Denmark), abortion continues. In short, the desire to control fertility does not mean automatic acceptance of contraception. Instead, it may prompt women to turn to abortion first. Even when the idea of contraception is accepted, abortion is likely to follow as a remedy for contraceptive failure, often high among those unaccustomed to using contraceptives and which, of course, occurs more frequently when contraception is carelessly practised, frequently the case when abortions are readily available; and of course, there is a small failure rate even with pills and IUDs. Since women tend to conceive more rapidly after an abortion than after childbirth, and can conceive more often in a given time period, the lack of contraception or its inefficient use is likely to result in a spiral of increased conceptions, increased abortions, further increases in conceptions, further increases in abortions, and so on, but only a gradual decrease in the number of births. [D.Callahan, 1970, p.290.]

The implication is that women resort increasingly to abortion because of the rise in contraceptive use rather than as an alternative. Once women see it as right and natural that they should control their own fertility, they are more likely to use contraceptives and to turn to abortion when contraceptive failure occurs. Besides, more frequent abortion will increase the chance of future fertility in this segment of the population.

It is not merely that an awareness of fertility control would tend to link contraceptive use and abortion but that increasingly sophisticated techniques of early termination will blur the distinction between the two. For instance, in America considerable debate centres around whether menstrual extraction is abortion or contraception.

It is our contention that the present rate of abortion in Britain will continue to rise. The stabilization of total numbers is a product of political decision and lack of facilities. Increased contraceptive use will add to, rather than minimize, the number for in no way is the potential demand for abortions being satisfied.

5.
The Reformers' Views

We have shown how the underlying model of society held by the reformers shapes the debate surrounding abortion. The theme is constantly repeated: the vast majority of 'normal' women neither need nor desire abortion; it is only those women who are marginal, whether it be physically, mentally or socially, who should be allowed abortion. Further, it is the practical concern of the reformers to aid these people, since reformist political philosophy aims to integrate the problem person into the body of the healthy society. In this fashion abortion is viewed as one of the means of ironing out the problems which society confronts.

But what are the assumptions which lead the reformists to expect little demand for abortion from the vast majority of women? There are four: related to the contraceptive revolution, to the rational character of procreation in present-day society, to the inviolable nature of the family and to the belief that all women necessarily want children.

The assumed widespread use of contraceptives fits these politics perfectly. Science allows rational sexual relationships, 'every child a wanted child' in the *vast majority* of cases. There is an element of truth in this. But contraceptives can mean pain, risk, and fears about future infertility and death. There are no perfect contraceptives.

Of those that exist the most efficient are used by the middle classes. The most popular form overall is the condom, used by half the total. 73 per cent of professional-class mothers take the pill – but just 37 per cent of other social classes. Working class women still often rely on methods like withdrawal which are unreliable [M.Bone, 1973] and are therefore more likely to need abortion services.

Even if effective contraceptives were equally distributed throughout the class structure the problem of unwanted children would remain. For a rational decision to have a child is dependent on the continuing existence of supportive relationships and adequate housing and finance. In no way, in a society characterized by a widespread re-evaluation of sexual relationships and where adequate material support is a problem, can a 'rational' decision at conception imply a rational decision at the time of birth. The social facilities which would facilitate such rationality are lacking.

The reformers' perspective does not question the family: abortion is seen as a means to maintain a strong family structure by eliminating births in those marginal groups where the family is already so large as to be threatened by an additional birth or where the individuals are considered psychologically or physically unable to support a stable family situation. Women outside these marginal categories are seen as automatically accepting childbirth without question and slipping into the traditional family structure. That they should question the need to have children or doubt the institutions that surround it, is not considered possible. For if the 'normal' woman does this, she is merely being frivolous or irresponsible and no rational legislator could consider such a demand.

So, abortion on demand is strongly resisted by the reformers because its existence would threaten their most cherished beliefs as to the nature of society. For to make abortion available because of economic circumstances would be to admit that the system is unable to provide women with a real choice regarding their family size. To concede that economic reasons drive so many women to seek abortions is to make a hefty indictment of the present social order. Further, to make abortion available to all women whatever their circumstances would be to admit that even when people are well enough off to afford children many will readily choose abortion. And this would undermine their conception of women and the family. It is because of their belief that the economic system and the nuclear family are fundamentally sane institutions in this best of all possible worlds, that the reformers deem women seeking abortion – outside of those in the most grim and marginal circumstances – to be not rational and to be acting frivolously.

So their opposition to 'frivolous' abortions (abortion on demand) is ideological. Their support for limited abortion is practical, a means of controlling social problems. Garret Hardin, for instance, writes:

> Is it good that a woman who does not want a child should bear one? An abundant literature of psychology and sociology proves that the unwanted child is a social danger. Unwanted children are more likely than others to grow up in psychologically unhealthy homes; they are more likely than others to become delinquents, and . . . when they become parents they are more likely than others to be poor parents themselves and breed another generation of unwanted children. This is a vicious circle if ever there was one. This is what an engineer would call positive feedback; it is ruinous to the social system. [G.Hardin, 1967, pp.82-83.]

It is not surprising that a link exists between broken homes and delinquency – but that does not mean broken homes are the *cause* of delinquency. The misery of the poor in cities breaks up homes, and shatters the family's members. It drives the children to crime, to vandalism. But it is poverty, material and emotional brought about by this system which creates broken homes and delinquency. It is reactionary nonsense to argue that inadequate families and weak personalities transmitted from generation to generation are the cause. It lumps all the blame on the individual and leaves the system alone.

In the eyes of the reformer the woman who needs an abortion is not only on the fringe of society. She is also literally, physically inadequate. Hindell and Simms quote approvingly from Sir Dugald Baird who wrote in 1969 about a 'sixth social class'. They are characterized he claimed:

> By early marriage, short stature, large number of children, high perinatal death rate from prematurity, and central nervous system

malformations, high infant death rates, and a high incidence of cancer of the cervix. Is this understood clearly enough by those responsible for the social services? [D.Baird, 1969.]

Clearly the poorest sector of the working class is perpetuated in misery from generation to generation. But it is not a 'closed class'. It is not a genetically based class, and the 'cycle of deprivation', as Sir Keith Joseph calls it, cannot be broken by using abortion to keep the population 'healthy'. To limit the population of this group, with all the fascist and racist implications that such a policy entails, would make no difference. In our kind of society certain individuals are always designated as social waste and would constantly replenish 'the sixth social class'.

This is not to deny that abortion alleviates the suffering of the very poor nor that close medical attention is required but merely to say that this is only one demand in a full programme of social change which would fundamentally alter their position. Further, the demand for abortion is far from limited to this group.

Limiting the demand for abortion to maladjusted and medically unfit groups avoids the ethical problems. The morality of the system being accepted, there is little place for a critical purchase outside of it, which would question its goals in any fundamental fashion. Thus the arguments concerning a woman's right to choose when to give birth or the implications of euthanasia with regard to the foetus, are subordinated to essentially *technical* questions. If the woman is medically unfit or psychologically traumatized then she is in no position to make choices; she is technically incapable to participate in the rational and ethical decisions of the more 'balanced' majority of the community. If the foetus is born into a maladjusted setting the child will, we are informed, be maladjusted itself – it will be a juvenile delinquent in the making.

Abortion for the reformers remains a therapeutic measure, and is correctly located in clinical judgements, but as Thomas Szasz aptly contends:

Abortion is a moral, not a medical problem. To be sure, the procedure is surgical; but this makes abortion no more a medical prob-

77

lem than the use of the electric chair makes capital punishment a problem of electrical engineering . . . The question is not one of medical and psychiatric justification for abortion, but of ethical judgement and social policy. If we truly believe that in a free society the expert should be on tap, not on top – we must place the power to decide when an abortion may be performed (legally) in the hands of the pregnant women, and not in the hands of the Church, the State, the American Medical Association, or the American Law Institute. [T.Szasz, 1966, p.148.]

It is quite clear. Our political and medical rulers bestow the possibility of an abortion on those they have elected to have problems. They do not respond to women's demands, or join in discussion about their rights. By maintaining that the demand for abortion arises from marginal groups, and not the broad stream of women they place themselves in a position from which the total demand appears to be small and fairly constant. Indeed, given their belief that an unwanted child, born in a problem family, would have a fair chance of creating a further problem family on reaching adulthood, and that abortion could break this cycle, they see the total demand for abortion as likely to decline in the long run. The provision of legal means of abortion is seen therefore not to necessitate radical restructuring of existing medical facilities but merely as a replacement for existing back-street operations.

We, however, would argue that the need for abortion is something that is likely to occur at least once in the lifetime of most women; the potential demand is enormous. Making abortion legal, however tentatively, opened a floodgate, which inevitably confounded both the cautious predictions and the politics of the reformers.

In our introduction we made the distinction between progressive and conservative reformers. The split between them became most apparent after the passing of the 1967 Act but it has been in evidence throughout the debate on abortion. ALRA is the body that can be most identified with progressive reformism although in the last few years, under the influence of the woman's movement, its position has been transformed. It now centres on a woman's right to choose. However, in the 'heroic' period of its history it belonged quite firmly in the reformist camp, and shared many of the fundamentals, if not the emphases, of the conservative reformers.

ALRA saw itself as a pressure group acting through parliament and believing in the possibility of achieving genuine abortion reform within the existing institutional framework. As Keith Hindell and Madeleine Simms (for a time General Secretary of ALRA) write in their history of abortion reform:

> When the argument is over and the reforms finally achieved surprises are in store for both sides. Aspects of the problem, that were previously hidden, are revealed for the first time; effects follow that were not entirely foreseen. . . . There is no one perfect solution, only a series of temporary and haphazard improvements, leading one to the other. These are the outward and visible signs of a living political democracy, and testify to the continuing urge towards personal freedom and individual decision which is the defining characteristic of a civilised society. [K.Hindell and M.Simms, 1971, p.244.]

That grave and continuing resistance to abortion reform should occur not haphazardly but as an inherent part of the system did not cross their minds; nor that drastic changes in the National Health Service would be necessary in order to achieve their aims.

The progressive reformers would not condone a separation between abortion as a medical problem and as a social and ethical problem. David Steel, author of the private member's Bill which became the 1967 Act, is critical of ALRA for making too much of the social reasons for abortion. In his foreword to Hindell and Simms' book, *Abortion Law Reformed*, he writes:

> In their desire to have retained a clear and separate 'social clause', I believe the authors underestimate the importance of the growing school of medical thought (of which Sir Dugald Baird is surely a founder member) that social conditions cannot be and ought not to be separated from medical considerations. I hope the Abortion Act by its very drafting has encouraged the concept of socio-medical care. [K.Hindell and M.Simms, 1971, p.7.]

79

In the event, ALRA was happy enough to concede amendments to the 1966 Bill – which firmly wedded the decision-making process to medical discretion – and Hindell and Simms quote approvingly Sir Dugald Baird's notion of the 'sixth social class'.

Thus both in their attitudes to parliamentary politics and the socio-medical nature of abortion ALRA were typically reformist. It is only when we turn to the question of which women need abortion that their major difference in emphasis with the conservatives becomes apparent.

The conservative reformers relegated demand to a restricted number of marginal groups, as we have shown. Lord Silkin, for example, when introducing the 1965 Abortion Bill, cited the following letter as an illustration of the typical woman requiring an abortion:

> Dear Lord Silkin,
> I am married to a complete drunk who is out of work more than he is in. I have four children and now at 40 I am pregnant again; I was just beginning to get on my feet, and get some of the things we needed. I've been working for the last three years, and cannot bear the thought of that terrible struggle to make ends meet again. I've tried all other methods that I've been told about; without success, so as a last resort I appeal to you – please help me if you possibly can. [K.Hindell and M.Simms, 1971, p.136.]

At times ALRA have agreed with this definition of need as when Hindell and Simms cite the socio-medical dictum of Dugald Baird, but they also went beyond it. Thus after their 1966 *Survey of Women*, they concluded:

> Thousands of women needed an abortion every year and most of them were prepared to ignore the criminal law in order to get one. The great majority of women never needed abortion but nevertheless favoured a change in the law so that all women could get skilled and legal abortions in almost all circumstances. [K.Hindell and M.Simms 1971, p.161.]

The demand for abortion stemmed not only from marginal groups but from the 'normal' woman's need for a second line of defence against unwanted pregnancy when contraception failed. [K.Hindell and M.Simms, 1971, p.16.] In fact, it was precisely the woman with a fully developed 'maternal instinct' who might require an abortion:

> Simms pointed out that whilst most women had a maternal instinct, at the same time they wished to have not more than two or three children, and they were appalled if they found they were having more children than they believed they could adequately care for. Should they accidentally become pregnant, they would then seek an abortion because of their feelings of responsibility to their husband and family, and because of their maternal instinct towards their existing children. [A.Hordern, 1971, p.15. See M.Simms, 'The Abortion Bill' (letter), *Lancet* 2, 384, 1967.]

So two categories of women were embraced by ALRA's concept of legitimate demand: (a) the marginal physical, psychological and social cases – the target population of the more conservative reformists; and (b) the 'normal' woman who used abortion as a long stop for contraceptive mistakes.

Simms with great candour describes these two categories as the 'deserving'. Since the 1967 Act, she notes, most of the 'deserving' obtain their abortions legally. 'But what', she asks, 'about the "undeserving"?'

> This somewhat Victorian distinction is not often employed nowadays, at least not openly . . . But, I think if we British abortion law reformers are honest with ourselves, we have to admit that the notion of the 'deserving' loomed large in our minds, and seemed to some of us, at least, to constitute the main justification for our activities. It was chiefly for the worn out mother of many children with an ill or illiterate or feckless or brutal or drunken or otherwise inadequate husband that we were fighting. We did not think very much in terms of the student, the nurse, the secretary, young, quite bright, literate, who got pregnant out of carelessness not ignorance. [M.Simms, 'Abortion and liberation', 1972, p.4.]

Thus, like all reformers, Madeleine Simms – probably the most articulate spokeswoman for ALRA – finds difficulty in granting abortion to the 'undeserving' 'normal' woman. Yet her search for the deep-seated irrationality which must lie behind the vast majority of abortions does not rest there. For it would seem that the seemingly 'normal' are 'abnormal' after all:

> quite a few of these seemingly 'undeserving' young women who queue up for abortions are themselves, on close investigation, found to come from unstable and insecure backgrounds that cannot dispose them towards a rational life style.

Moreover:

> because of these disturbed backgrounds, they are unlikely to make good mothers themselves until they have had time to mature and stabilise, and that to force them to have children before they are ready for this experience, is the perfect recipe for producing a new generation of inadequate or disturbed children. In so far as it does this society is itself behaving as irrationally as those young women on whom it is trying to prevail . . . The result is that, by compelling such women to have babies against their better judgement, society damages itself. These babies, as recent cost-benefit studies show, are among the most expensive to bring up, since they have disproportionate recourse to the state's welfare services. They are also much more likely to come to grief themselves as juvenile delinquents and in other ways damaging to society. [M.Simms, 'Abortion and liberation', 1972, p.4.]

Simms has produced here a masterpiece of reformist rhetoric. No normal rational woman would require an abortion unless she were (a) destroyed by circumstances (by definition, only a few people), (b) had experienced a contraceptive failure (by definition, a declining occurrence). But what of the others who seem rational? Have we opened the legal floodgates to a spate of abortions for even 'rational' women? No, for here Simms turns to 'scientific research' which reveals that they too come from disturbed backgrounds and even worse will create disturbed children and so put at risk the attempts at social engineering. Leaving aside, for the moment, the scientific credibility of such statements, let us note that they allow reformism's basic premises concerning human nature and the social order to remain unchallenged. The language is that of an élite which thinks in terms of what they, as an elite, will *bestow* upon the deserving. It was not until the women's movement fully entered the debate that the language changed to what they, a mass movement, demanded for *themselves*.

Thus although ALRA's traditional policy called for a significantly enlarged number of people to make demands on the abortion services, it in no way suggested complete abortion on demand. It purposely excluded 'normal' women without children or with one child for that matter. It linked its aims directly to the maintenance of the nuclear family. As Madeleine Simms commented in 1972:

> most members of ALRA did not think of abortion as a means to some quite other end, nor did they desire to destroy the nuclear family. Indeed, they argued that by civilising and humanising the abortion issue, family life would be strengthened. [*ibid.* p.1.]

Their difference in emphasis explains why the two wings of reformers made such different estimates of the likely demand for abortion. The conservative reformers, like James White, expected the legal abortion rate to be small and easily catered for within the NHS, except for a small fringe of private practice which would allow personal choice, as in other spheres of medicine. As we have seen, they were surprised by the numbers and quickly realized that the situation they had feared had come about. 'Normal' women were making use of the facilities, to a greater extent than the marginal groups for which they had hoped to cater. ALRA, in contrast, holding to the figure of 100,000 illegal abortions prior to the 1967 Act, explained all these cases as marginal. They interpreted the peaking of the legal abortion figures at just over 100,000 as a demonstration of the Act's success in transferring abortions from the illegal to the legal sector. In truth, it was the conservative reformists, however unpalatable their views, who displayed the greater insight.

6.
The Anti-Abortionist Backlash

The image of society, and of women, held by the promoters and supporters of the 1967 Act did not correspond to reality. The result was an abortion boom, a failing NHS and a growing private sector – which catered for the better off. Lack of facilities meant that terminations occurred later than was desirable, which led to the risk of depression and trauma, and emphasized the ethical problem of abortion.

They had hoped for a cut in profiteering and medical malpractice. The result was more profiteering, and accusations of semi-legal practices. Massive gains had been made as a result of the Act. But the problems were public – and equally massive. Some women, the better off, could, it seemed, gain 'abortion on demand'.

The result was a split between the conservative and progressive reformers, but, even more important, the accumulation of political capital out of which the anti-abortionists could create a mass movement. The inadequacies of reformism provided the substance on which anti-abortionism thrived.

The concept of socio-medical criteria embraced by the reformers placed a considerable amount of power in the hands of the doctors. What the reformers considered to be a technical decision was interpreted by the medical profession as an ethical one. Sections of the profession, particularly at the consultant level, opted out by using the conscience clause. This intensified the pressure on public facilities elsewhere and produced a situation in which doctors and medical staff in more liberal hospitals were often alienated by the pressure and degree of specialization required in abortion operations. General practitioners, on the other hand, involved more directly with their patients' problems and fixing gladly on the changing balance of risk between abortion and pregnancy, interpreted the 1967 Act liberally.

These consequences – all of which would have been obviated if abortion on demand were available in the public sector – were latched on to by the anti-abortionists. For it enabled them to supplement their moral arguments with a series of arguments based on the failures of the 1967 Act. Ironically it is the shortcomings of the reform which provided the political arguments for the anti-abortionists.

SPUC opposes abortion. Although its more liberal wing would allow abortions in those increasingly rare cases where the mother's life is endangered by childbirth, its view of the social order differs from that of the reformers in that its members do not see a gradual progress towards social harmony backed by a series of progresses in legislation. Although they have no quarrel with the fundamental basis of the social order, they view the problems which do occur as a product of bad government and leadership, particularly those of a reformist variety. They are therefore critical of what they see as 'the rising tide of permissiveness' and the moral laxity of the modern world. Their central theme is the corruption of standards by a small cynical élite and the absence of moral leadership by those in legitimate authority.

Thus Mary Whitehouse, writing in 1966, noted:

Permissive reforms are now being pushed through Parliament one by one. Although they command support from vocal minorities, it would be a mistake to believe they represent the wish of the majority of ordinary people. And it is becoming more and more clear that the motivating group behind them are the British Humanist Association, the National Secular Society, the Homosexual Law Reform Society and the Abortion Law Reform Society. No one denies these groups the right to work for these things if they choose . . . But no one has given the BBC a mandate to promote their causes. [M.Whitehouse, 1967, p.167.]

SPUC repeatedly quotes opinion polls to show that a majority of people in the country are in agreement with them. Why, then, do so many women choose to have abortions? The reasons SPUC gives are:

(a) demoralisation: the pregnant woman is in a weak position and is pressurised into abortion by her doctor, her husband, parents or lover.
(b) corruption: the permissive élite propagandise their facilities through 'charitable' bodies behind which lurk touts and profiteers.
(c) promiscuity: the unmarried girl, in particular, is bombarded with propaganda which encourages the immediate gratification of sexual desire rather than the building of genuine loving relationships centering on marriage and the family.

SPUC uses this idea of corruption to explain why the 1967 legislation occurred, and why women avail themselves of it. The notorious book *Babies for Burning* [M.Litchfield and S.Kentish, 1974] which became another bible for SPUC members, is interesting not only for its numerous inaccuracies [see: O.Gillie, M.Wallace, P.Ashdown-Sharp, *Sunday Times*, 30 March 1975, p.2.] but also for its imagery:

it was . . . American money that was used to get the British abortion industry off the ground. The whole push for the 1967 Abortion Act was American-inspired. The money that was thrown about in the right quarters came to a fortune. The big spenders knew they would retrieve their speculative investments a thousand times. [Whitehouse, p.174.]

As, in their view, no sane parliament could pass such an Act, it was inspired by foreign corruption. But what of the doctors themselves who work in the private abortion sector?

Psychologists are adamant that the avid pro-abortionists have fascist tendencies. This was evident from our inquiries . . . Selective killing – which abortion is – and selective breeding, were Hitler's brain children. [*ibid.* p.181.]

It is useless, of course, to enter into debate at this level but it is significant that Nazi policies were adamantly anti-abortionist and that the psychologists who link pro-abortion support to fascist attitudes are precisely those who have continuously argued for the genetic basis of racial inequality.

Further, if these doctors are not motivated by Nazi ideology, it is naked profit and professional incompetence that has brought them into the business:

> The abortion agencies are the start of the death queue. This is where the conveyor belt begins its swift and irrevocable journey to the furnace. They are very conscious of their role. If they let a pregnant girl get out of their grasp, it is less money in the bank for them and less money in the bank for the 'butchers' in the clinics. Suffice it to say that very few women do get away. The programming and high-pressure salesmanship, almost tantamount to bullying, is too sophisticated and watertight for more than a few 'flies' to escape the net.
>
> No other section of medicine has attracted such a motley crew of pirates . . . Abortion is the 'black sheep' of medicine. Many of the doctors working in the twilight world could not find jobs elsewhere. Putting it bluntly, they are the 'deadbeats' of their profession. Most of them are bereft of ambition. They are left with the empty philosophy of the 'fast buck'. [*ibid.* pp.24-25.]

It is not that the women want abortions:

> we begin to learn something of the frightening truth about the way girls are often blinkered, blindfolded and fooled to enable affluent men to become richer. Pregnant and frightened girls are lured, coaxed and snared into a net that holds so many dangers, both mental and physical. [*ibid.* p.110.]

This is corruption imagery in perfection! No legislation would have occurred without alien influences, no genuine doctor would be involved in the operation, no woman who had not been pressured would want an abortion. Let us note, at this point, that such a picture of the world is common wherever events occur which suggest that there might be something fundamentally wrong in the social order. Thus, a strike of any duration is usually depicted in the media as the result of the *irrationality* of workers, exacerbated perhaps by *mismanagement* by particular segments of the managerial staff, and *exploited* by a small group of politically motivated men. No decent worker would strike, runs the moral, because there is little really wrong with the position of workers in this society.

This is not a view which the James Whites or the David Steels would completely share. There are problems – but on the fringe. However, the idea that the vast majority of women might want the right to abortion would be considered irrational by SPUC, James White *and* David Steel.

The practical result is that when the Act was seen to be catering for more than the 'fringe' it was not just SPUC which complained. Parliament as a whole were quite happy to blame profiteers and 'psychopathic' doctors.

None of this is to deny that profiteering takes place – it does so throughout private practice. Yet at no point do SPUC and its supporters suggest that the private sector be abolished and sufficient NHS facilities be provided. Their fundamental assumption is that abortion is a violation of the life of the unborn child. Complaints about 'profiteering' are then added like icing on the cake. Even if the 'excesses' were removed SPUC would still oppose abortion.

By spotlighting the profiteering part of the private sector SPUC suggests that only 'bent' doctors will involve themselves in the business and that the majority of 'normally' motivated doctors are against abortion. This scarcely accords with the sterling work of doctors within the National Health Service and with the elementary fact that it was the liberal interpretation of the 1967 Act by a host of GPs which created the situation which SPUC so abhors.

Even more than the reformers, SPUC maintains that the 'real' demand for abortion is small. They believe the estimates of illegal abortions prior to 1967 to be greatly exaggerated, and, even more untenably, that legalization of abortion does not affect, or increase, the number of illegal abortions:

Constant experience has been that when laws are liberalized, the legal abortion rate skyrockets, the illegal abortion rate does not drop, but frequently also rises. The reason constantly given is the relative lack of privacy of the official procedures (Europe, Japan, Colorado, etc). [Dr and Mrs J.C.Wilkie, 1972.]

For SPUC, the rise in abortions after the 1967 Act was a product of corrupting influences. From their perspective, there is no deeply felt need for abortion amongst the majority of women, it is the pernicious effect of the legislation and the agencies that it gave rise to that has created the problem. The solution is simple: to repeal the Abortion Act or amend it out of existence. If that were done, the following dire consequences of the Act would be severely curtailed:

1. Profiteering and quasi-legal activities;
2. the rising demand for abortion;
3. physical morbidity accompanying abortion;
4. post-abortion trauma;
5. the killing of 'live' foetuses.

Ironically enough, all these consequences would be intensified if the anti-abortionists' aims were successful. Thus:

1. The demand would not disappear but would revert to the illegal sector. Prices would soar, and profits rise. The sophisticated techniques which large-scale abortion under the Act has engendered would not simply disappear but would remain to be utilized by the illegal sector, which would make more money faster and more systematically than ever before.

2. The demand for abortion relates to deep-seated and probably increasing problems of women.

3. Illegal abortions would mean that termination occurred later than they do now and under less savoury medical conditions. Morbidity would, therefore, increase.

4. The trauma surrounding abortion relates, in part, to the prevalent morality surrounding its occurrence. Abortion on demand as an accepted practice would reduce much self-doubt, guilt and anxiety amongst women. Illegal abortions would intensify it and, further, because of the later termination make psychological trauma all the more likely.

5. The ethical problems surrounding abortion are consider-

able and linked to problems of euthanasia. They certainly cannot be solved as both SPUC and the reformers would have it, by recourse to rival groups of doctors each of which claims authority to determine when the onset of 'life' occurs. Decisions about the maintenance of life are made by the medical profession and hospital authorities daily. The choice between investing in equipment to deal with minor ailments and spending money on intensive-care cardiac equipment is an obvious example. At all times questions of cost, limited resources and the ability to pay for treatment are faced throughout medical practice not only in the sphere of abortion. After all, any life could be prolonged if sufficient money were available. It is of utmost priority that such decisions are made democratically in the interest of the community and not left in the hands of either the medical professions or a hospital bureaucracy.

Our aim should be to create a society which is egalitarian in its medical care and which provides for the full social development of its members. To value human life is not to insist that women must be cast inevitably in the role of childbearers if conception has occurred, nor is it to demand that unwanted children be brought into the world. It is misleading to talk about the potentiality for life. The potentiality for producing offspring has been infinitely increased by modern medical science. But so also has the potentiality for choice. Not so long ago the SPUC leaders, who are now opposing abortion as an ungodly interference with the potential for life, were opposing the use of contraceptives for the same reason. Having lost that battle they have simply retrenched themselves in the abortion debate.

6. The complaints about 'fully formed foetuses' are a further irrelevancy. Fully formed or not the anti-abortionists would oppose their termination. Further, it is precisely restrictive policies which result in late termination. Early pregnancy testing coupled with adequate abortion facilities would blur the present distinction between contraception and abortion. Except in very few instances they would make non-problematic the ethical question unless contraception itself were resuscitated as a moral issue. But it is exactly

90

such an advance that SPUC would resist; and it is the latter dead debate which it would be only too glad to revive. Even in terms of present contraceptive practice it is interesting to note that intra-uterine devices blur the boundary between contraception and abortion as one of its modes of action is to abort the fertilized egg.

Thus on every point SPUC would create legislation which would exacerbate their complaints and doubts about abortion. It would be easy to portray this as an irrational outburst of moral indignation but it is more than this. It is a perfectly reasonable conclusion derived from invalid conceptions of women and the social order.

Let us now turn to discuss the measures which SPUC would advocate to deal with the increase in population that would result from their policies. Here they are very astute in detecting the weaknesses in the reformers' position:

1. Population explosion. The reformers will argue that eco-logical pressures undercut any moral stance against abortion. There are simply too many people on 'this crowded island'. To this SPUC has a simple and correct answer. It points to the declining birth rate over the last six years.

2. Social engineering. The reformers centre their argument on alleviating the plight of the socially marginal who are unable to bring up a child or further children properly. For the anti-abortionists this is nonsense:

> Choosing abortion as a solution to social problems would seem to indicate that certain individuals and groups of individuals are attempting to maximise their own comforts by enforcing their own prejudices. As a result, pregnant schoolgirls continue to be ostrac-ised, mothers of handicapped children are left to fend for them-selves, and the poor are neglected in their struggle to attain equal conditions of life. And the *only* solution offered these people is abortion . . .
>
> We must move towards creating a society in which material pur-suits are not the ends of our lives; where no child is hungry or neglected . . . Instead of destroying life, we should destroy the con-ditions which make life intolerable. [Dr and Mrs J.C.Wilkie, 1972.]

More 'freedom for women' can simply mean 'less protection'. When a baby would be inconvenient, a mother can now come under strong pressure from the father or from relatives, to apply for abortion, and in many cases does so. Pressure at such a time can be difficult to resist, if the mother is financially dependent. [SPUC *'Need we kill 450 every day?'*]

Can bad housing and overcrowding really justify killing the unborn? What a negative solution! No. The right way, because the positive way, is to tackle the bad housing and to give immediate relief to the mother-to-be who just has not got space for a newcomer. If this sounds smug we should recall the range of welfare and social workers ready to help the needy, and the facilities which they have at their disposal. [J.J.Scarisbrick, 1971, pp.27-28.]

The arguments for abortion as a form of population control to prevent overcrowding are simply wrong. In the 1960s successive British governments encouraged immigration to meet the demands of the labour market. At present, unemployment is the product of an economy which functions badly, not of overcrowding. More important, population control is not in practice directed at the total population. but at the social casualties of the system. SPUC senses this. It launches itself on the woman pressurized into abortion against her will; on workers fobbed off by abortion as a surrogate for material gain.

But to detect weaknesses is not to solve them. For there is precious little that organizations such as SPUC would provide for women or the poor other than charity. It is true that a woman's dependent position renders her liable to pressures which limit her choice whether or not to have children. But abortion on demand is a step towards breaking from such dependency. SPUC bemoans the dependency yet produces proposals that would forge her chains. The same might be said of the poor. It is true that the reformers' concern with population control and their attempts to iron out social problems through piecemeal reforms such as the 1967 Act are lamentable. Yet to berate their aims is not to deny the gains which abortion represents to the working class. It is by welding free abortion on demand to the whole range of changes necessary to generate genuine freedom of choice that we transcend reformism. It is by rejecting the reformers' programme of limited abortion for socially isolated women and the lower working class that we recognize the fundamental problems faced by all women and the whole working class. SPUC cannot begin to do so.

7.
The Limits of Reformism

The goal of the reformers is to provide abortion facilities for those women deemed incapable of caring for a child or additional children. The reformers resist most strongly the pressure for abortion on demand. The irony of their position is that the restrictive legislation and facilities which they advocate is best exploited by those women who are well-off and have the know-how to find for themselves appropriate abortion facilities, women who, they suggest, are likely to have an abortion for 'frivolous' reasons, and who are not in dire social and psychological straits. For these women the reformers have helped to engineer an approximation of abortion on demand; a cruel irony, for this is precisely what they had sought to avoid.

There is, of course, a simple way out of the predicament: to concede the demand for free, widely available abortion on the NHS, as happened with contraception, for precisely the same reasons.

The response of the government in the present crisis has not been encouraging. It has been to cut back on 'non-essential' spending, with NHS abortion facilities an obvious target in their terms, even though the declining labour market and the extreme pressures on the social services point in the opposite direction. For an abortion costs considerably less than maternity, let alone educational and welfare facilities. But could there be a change in the reformers' attitudes to abortion in lines with the economic interests of the ruling class?

The basic problem is the conflict between their practical

aims and their ideology. For to concede abortion on demand threatens, as we have shown, their beliefs regarding both the economy and the nature of women. Yet situations do arise, particularly at times of crisis, where the most hallowed beliefs of the rulers are tempered by their economic and political interests. In October 1974, for example, the Conservative Shadow Minister of Health made the following notorious remarks about birth control :

> The balance of our population, our human stock is threatened. A recent article . . . showed that a high and rising proportion of children are being born to mothers least fitted to bring children into the world and bring them up. They are born to mothers who were first pregnant in adolescence in social classes four and five. Many of these girls are unmarried, many are deserted or divorced or soon will be. Some are of low intelligence, most of low educational attainment.
>
> They are unlikely to be able to give children the stable emotional background . . . which are more important than riches. They are producing problem children, the future unmarried mothers, delinquents, denizens of our borstals, subnormal educational establishments, prisons, hostels for drifters. Yet these mothers, the under-20s in many cases, single parents, from classes four and five, are now producing a third of all births. A high proportion of these births are a tragedy for the mother, the child and for us.
>
> Yet what shall we do? If we do nothing, the nation moves towards degeneration, however much resources we pour into preventative work and the overburdened educational system . . .
>
> Yet proposals to extend birth control facilities to these classes of people, particularly the young unmarried girls, the potential young unmarried mothers, evokes entirely understandable moral opposition. Is it not condoning immorality? I suppose it is. But which is the lesser evil, until we are able to remoralise whole groups and classes of people, undoing the harm done when already weak restraints on strong instincts are further weakened by permissiveness in television, in films, on bookstalls? [*The Times*, 21 October 1974.]

On that occasion Sir Keith Joseph's concern about conventional sexual morality obviously took second place to his fears of over-breeding by the lower orders. Is it possible for the debate about abortion to be transformed in this fashion? The introduction

95

of a comparatively liberal abortion law in New York indicates that it is indeed possible.

In 1970, New York State passed one of the most permissive abortion laws in the western world. Abortion was legalized on the request of the patient, provided she was not more than 24 weeks pregnant and the operation was performed by a licensed physician. There followed a dramatic change: in two years more than 400,000 women had legal abortions. Over 60 per cent of this total consisted of non-residents who came from less liberal states. The full impact of the legislation can be gauged by the fact that it took five years after passing of the 1967 Act for abortions in the whole of Britain to reach this figure. Beneficial effects were immediate and progressive, as we see below:

Table 3. New York Resident Abortions by Time and Method of Termination

	1971-72 %	1972-73 %
Abortions carried out in first 12 weeks of pregnancy	73	82
Abortions carried out in 21 weeks or later of pregnancy	4	2.5
Abortions carried out by vacuum aspiration	47	68

Sources: C.Tietze, 1973, pp.36-41; M.Simms, 1973, pp.252-253.

Abortions which had previously resulted in a high mortality rate because of their illegality, became, in this short period, a remarkably safe operation. Thus an extremely low mortality rate of 3.5 per 100,000 abortions was achieved which could usefully be contrasted to the British rate of 8 per 100,000 – itself a very low figure when compared to a maternity mortality rate of 14 per 100,000.

Because abortions were legal most of them occurred in the first twelve weeks of pregnancy and increasingly so, as facilities and knowledge of their availability expanded. Moreover simple vacuum aspiration techniques could be used, because of the early termination. As Christopher Tietze comments:

> Of greater importance than the personal characteristics of women, and more important even than the circumstances under which the abortions were performed, is the period of gestation at which the pregnancies were terminated. Abortions in the second trimester (13 weeks or more) are associated with a much higher incidence of complications, including fatal complications, than abortions in the first trimester (12 weeks or earlier). In addition, late abortions, especially those after 20 weeks of gestation, may involve emotional stress for the pregnant woman as well as for such other persons involved as the nurses attending the expulsion of a relatively large and well-developed fetus. [Tietze, *op. cit.* p.37.]

What happened to make such a liberal reform possible in New York?

First was the exacerbation of the 'urban crisis'. 'Urban crisis' is a constant theme of American politics. That the richest society in human history cannot provide employment for its poor, cannot provide the most elementary level of public services, cannot protect its citizens against the crime which ravages its streets, is a contradiction of the most enormous proportions, and one which cannot easily be brushed under a carpet of 'inevitable social progress'. It is a crisis of confidence in the system which demands more radical reforms, and a rethinking of hallowed beliefs and practices. Abortion law reform in New York was primarily an attempt to ameliorate the problems of the ghetto – delinquency, 'overpopulation', welfare costs – and as such was a classic use of social engineering techniques.

In times of crisis reformism can shift its position: it can admit that it is not just at the extreme margins of society where problems occur, it can extend its net further into the lower working class and it can demand more 'radical' solutions. In the context of the present economic crisis in Britain, with the increase in social problems which this gives rise to, it is inconceivable that reformism would be able to renegotiate its terms of reference.

The second factor in New York's permissive abortion legislation, was the large, politically-conscious women's movement. The scale of concessions such a movement can force out of the legislature is dependent on its political power (and in New York State this is considerable, even on the level of voting) and the degree to which the interests of government itself lie in this direction. In crisis situations government interests do veer in a reformist direction. This does not mean that the women's movement is co-opted by the legislature, but that all reform wrested out of the ruling class is, outside of a revolutionary situation, shaped and altered in the directon of the ruling interests. To argue, for example, that the Factory Acts were simply a direct expression of ruling class interest in that they provided a healthier and, therefore, more productive labour force would be simplistic in the extreme; as it would be to deny that significant legislative gains have been made in areas such as health, housing and race relations as a result of the political pressures of the labour movement. But of course, the resources for, and limits and implementation of, such legislation are undeniably shaped by ruling class interests.

Lastly, in times of crisis reformism can find itself with strange political bedfellows. In New York one of the major sources of support for the legislation was Governor Rockefeller. His family, the founders of Standard Oil, have been involved for decades in family planning in an effort to control the threat of unrest in the Third World, caused – they believe – by 'overpopulation'. By 1970 Rockefeller had turned his attention to the United States itself. It takes little imagination to comprehend how the political right in America both fears the rise in the black population and are willing to discard cherished beliefs in order to cut its birthrate.

The criticisms of this reform came from two sources: the feminist and the black movements.

Feminist groups argued that despite the liberalization, the medical profession still monopolized the practice of abortion. What was needed was decriminalization of abortion so that women could, without hindrance, create self-help groups in this field and develop extremely cheap abortions performed with the minimum of fuss and professional interference.

The black movement criticized the abortion reform from precisely the opposite viewpoint. The 1970 legislation was greeted by the Black Panther Party as follows.

Black People know that part of our revolutionary strength lies in the fact that we outnumber the pigs – and the pigs realise this too. This is why they are trying to eliminate as many people as possible before they reach their inevitable doom.

The decision (to liberalise the abortion laws) will be based on the feelings of the woman and her doctor. The struggle for 'Women's Liberation' via a woman's prerogative to eliminate an unwanted child has won a victory. But a victory for whom? Perhaps it is a victory for the white middle class mother who wants to have a smaller family, thereby enabling her to have more material goods or more time to participate in whatever fancies her at the moment. But most of all it is a victory for the oppressive ruling class who will use this law to kill off Black and other oppressed people before they are born. To the Black woman . . . it is an announcement of death before birth. Black women love children, and now in order to see to it that they do not starve . . . that they do not have to suffer all the degradation of this racist, capitalist society, they will kill them before they are born. Black women love large families and the only reason that they would eliminate them is to rid them of the pain and agony of trying to survive. Why in a country where farmers . . . who are given large sums of public funds to not grow food; where food is actually burned, must Black mothers kill their unborn children . . . Absurd! Eliminating ourselves is not the solution to the hunger problem in America, nor any other problem that could exist from a so-called unwanted pregnancy in the context of a capitalist society. The solution lies in overthrowing the system and returning the means of production back to the people . . .

Black women will reject this 'legalised murder' just as they rejected the attempt to force family planning in the guise of pills and coils.

99

> And for those who say it will prevent useless deaths and per-
> manent injury to those women driven to self-inflicted abortion,
> based on capitalistic morality, or for those who have legitimate
> physical and mental reasons; we say that an Abortion Law doesn't
> ensure good hospital treatment . . . We say Black people are not
> able to trust these slaughter houses to perform such delicate opera-
> tions. [*Black Panther*, 4 July 1970, p.2.]

We have quoted this extract at length because its position
will be unfamiliar to most European socialists and feminists. Yet
its antagonism to population control is repeated by countless
Third World socialists and it is important that we appraise its argument, in order to understand the contradictions contained within
the movement for abortion reform and the inter-relationship between the birth control and population control movements, issues
we take up in the next chapter.

If New York showed how reformism responded permissively
under the pressure of urban crisis, Japan illustrates how reformism
is attempting to revert from its permissive phase. It is an important
case in warning us against the flexible and infinitely re-negotiable
nature of reformist concessions, responding as they do to the
changing material interests of the ruling class in particular periods.
It alerts us to the need to relate the gains won from government to
the political compromises that they are willing to make in the
direction of their own interests, and to the ever-present danger that
permissive legislation may be rescinded.

Pre-war Japan followed a typically fascist policy on childbirth: 'Have babies, increase our prosperity!', was the slogan.
After the war reconstruction demanded a strict limitation on the
population which resulted in the 1948 Eugenic Protection Law.
Together with the amendments of 1949 and 1952 this law allowed
abortion for economic reasons provided the permission of a certi-
fied doctor was obtained. The objections from ultra-nationalists
and religious groups were quelled at the time by reference to the
dire need for population control. In the late 1960s Japan once
again experienced a nationalist resurgence and government policy

began to change. In 1967 the Minister of Health and Welfare launched a campaign against Japan as an 'abortion paradise'. In 1968 a White Paper on public welfare announced: 'Now that the national income has increased, it is time to consider prohibiting abortion for economic reasons.' On 11 May 1973 – for the third time in four years – the government introduced a bill in the Diet to amend the Eugenic Protection Law. Taken as a whole the reform aimed at prohibiting abortion for economic reasons, at lowering the age at which women could legally have children, and at encouraging abortion in the case of 'handicapped' mothers.

Opposition to the amendment came from the trade unions, the women's liberation movement, and the Aoishiba-no-kai – a group of cerebral palsy victims and their supporters. Sohyo (the General Council of Japanese Trade Unions) declared the principle cause of abortions to be low wages, housing shortages and lack of childcare facilities. 'The government should take measures to solve these social problems instead of revising the present law.' [cited in N.Yoshiko, 1973, p.15.]

The women's liberation movement opposed the change for attempting to reinforce the ties between women and the nuclear family and for emphasizing the role of women as primarily that of childbearers. They doubted that the amendment would actually decrease the number of abortions because of the loopholes in the Act and the liberal attitudes of the medical profession. The aim of the change in their views was primarily ideological:

> The aim of the reform law is not to decrease abortions – to insure an adequate labour supply, say – but to shift the 'blame' for abortion from society (which in itself necessitates abortions for economic reasons) to the individual woman. The reform bill which would substitute the 'mental health' of the mother for 'economic reasons' carries the implications that women who have abortions are not psychologically normal or are 'easy women' who have deviated from public morality. [Yoshiko p.18.]

They point to a very pertinent issue here, namely that legislation can have an ideological component which is often more important than its actual effect. While there is considerable confusion and debate within the Japanese ruling class as to whether or not the population is optimal to meet labour demands, there is unanimity that abortion for economic reasons is an anachronism and a national disgrace in the new Japan. To relabel the legislation, therefore, has a significance whether or not any dramatic changes in the abortion rate occurs. In this the women's movement is confirming Joseph Gusfield's thesis in his important study of the prohibition movement in the United States [J.R.Gusfield, 1963] namely, that the symbolic degradation of those whom reformers deem 'deviant' or 'feckless' often overshadows the instrumental potency of the legislation.

The third group prominent in the struggle were the league of the cerebral palsied whose position is unique in contemporary abortion movements in Japan and extremely significant. For the Aoishiba-no-kai oppose the 'liberal' concessions made to the handicapped:

> The reform bill denies the right of the 'handicapped' to live. It fails to put first things first. It is the urgent task of government to create a society where those who are born as the 'handicapped' do not feel unhappy. [ibid. p.16.]

In their opposition to the amendment and their counterposing the demand to de-criminalize abortion by dissolving the Eugenic Protection Act itself, the Japanese movement has shown extreme sophistication. It constantly stresses that abortion is a woman's right to choose, but that real choice is absent in a system which *necessitates* abortion for many women. To place the blame back on the system at a time when reformism wishes to reassert the marginal and individual causes of the phenomenon, is a significant achievement.

8.
The Politics of Population Control

A farmer, gently stroking his young son's hair, told me: 'These Americans are enemies of the smile on this child's face. All they are interested in is war or family planning.' [M.Mamdani, 1972, p.147.]

Malthus . . . asserts that population constantly exerts pressure on the means of subsistence; that as production is increased, population increases in the same proportion; and that the inherent tendency of population to multiply beyond the available means of subsistence is the cause of all poverty and vice. For if there are too many people then in one way or another they must be eliminated; they must die, either by violence or through starvation. When this has happened, however, a gap appears once more, and this is immediately filled by other propagators of population, so that the old poverty begins anew. Moreover, this is the case under all conditions . . . The savages of New Holland, who live one to the square mile, suffer just as much from overpopulation as England. In short, if we want to be logical, we have to recognise that the earth was already over-populated when only one man existed. Now the consequences of this theory is that since it is precisely the poor who constitute this surplus population, nothing ought to be done for them, except to make it as easy as possible for them to starve to death; to convince them that this state of affairs cannot be altered and that there is no salvation for their entire class other than that they should propagate as little as possible; or that if this is not practicable, it is at any rate better that a state institution for the painless killing of the children of the poor should be set up . . . each working class family being allowed two and half children, and the excess being painlessly destroyed. [R.Meek, *Marx and Engels on Malthus*, 1953, p.59.]

Here we have Engels, at his most ironical, lampooning Malthusianism: 'this vile doctrine, this blasphemy against man and nature'.

103

Population planning is the twentieth century version of Malthusianism. Its message is the same – that overpopulation is the prime cause of poverty – but its message is more optimistic, less fatalistic, namely that adroit family planning can lessen humanity's ills.

It is also a worldwide political programme. The United States Agency for International Development (AID) provides more than one half of the Third World's population control budget. The amounts involved are large: $250 million from 1968 to 1971, $225 million authorized for fiscal years 1972 and 1973. [B.Mass, 1972, p.8.]

AID provides support to the huge International Planned Parenthood Federation (IPPF) with its 72 affiliates. Its trustees include Eugene R. Black (Director of the Chase Manhattan Bank) and Lamont du Pont Copeland (Director of Du Pont) and has had as honorary chairman such progressive thinkers as Dwight D. Eisenhower.

IPPF is a direct descendant of the eugenics movement on the one hand, the feminist birth control movement on the other – a mixture of reactionary and progressive strands. [see B.Mass, 1972, L.Gordon, 1974.]

In an important essay on the control of human reproduction, Linda Gordon points to these two poles of thought which existed throughout the last century:

A sharper form (of class difference) can be seen . . . between the population control and the birth control movements. The distinction between these two movements, not widely understood, is essentially this: 'birth control' . . . has referred to reproductive self-determination by individual women or couples for individual purposes; 'population control' has referred to a large-scale social policy of limiting births throughout a whole society or in certain social groups for the purpose of changing economic, political and/or ecological conditions. Modern population control thought began with Malthusian economics and the argument that population surplus kept the poor poor. Within the birth control movement, population ideas were often presented simultaneously with demands for women's reproductive self-determination. At times population control ideas dominated, stimulating resistance from those who perceived them as justifying inequality and exploitation. [L.Gordon, 1974, p.62.]

The two poles of the debate are often blurred, not only because of the considerable power and money which has backed population control, but also because both views can be made to fit together in a false yet insidious fashion.

Birth control focuses on individual choice. Population control is concerned with decisions on the level of the total society. It is all too easy for the advocate of birth control to heartily endorse women's rights and then, when turning to the more airy problems of the nature of society as a whole, back up their arguments with the proposition that what is good for the individual woman by a happy coincidence produces effects which make sense for the total social framework. It is only when we look at the world from a socialist position that the contradictions between the struggle of individuals for freedom of fertility and sexuality and the repressive nature of the social organization *as it is* becomes apparent. Similarly, it is all too easy for left-wing critics of population planning to spiral down to the individual woman and condemn her struggle for self-determination as something which naively plays into the hands of the system.

The theory behind population control is neo-Malthusian, which states that the cause of poverty and civil unrest lies in the voracious tendency of population to devour surplus. It places the finger of responsibility on the 'feckless' individual rather than the system. It is an ideological weapon of the first order: it can be used to convince individuals that they might advance their material position without any need to change society; it allows the labour force to be tailored to the demands of the present economic system; it promises to change everything without in fact changing anything.

In practice, it is seldom *all* populations which the controllers would like to see reduced. Mamdani describes how Paul Ehrlich, author of the popular tract *The Population Bomb*, was made aware of the 'population problem'. It dawned on him 'one stinking

Table 4. Birth Control and Population Control

	Birth Control	Population Control
Theoretical Base	Feminism and socialism	Neo-Malthusianism
Arbiter of Decision	Individual woman or couple	An elite of experts who must convince the population
Aim of Control	1. Woman's control of her fertility	1. Economic development without fundamental change
	2. The separation of sexuality from procreation	2. The eugenic elimination of the unfit
Proposed Effects of Control	1. The prevention of immiseration and brutalisation	1. The control of urban unrest and political dissatisfaction
	2. Provide the economic and sexual *basis* for the liberation of women	2. The prevention of war, starvation
Effect on the Individual	A crucial break in dependency	Economic self-help and advancement
Targets of the Movement	All women	Third World and socially marginal people
Place in a Programme for Social Change	As one step within a general programme of fundamental change	As a panacea which will solve social problems without fundamental change in the system

hot night in Delhi' while driving through by taxi, when he and his companions became terrified by the mass of people swirling around them. Mamdani comments:

> The fact is that a hot summer night on Broadway in New York or Piccadilly Circus in London would put Ehrlich in the midst of a far larger crowd. Yet such an experience would not spur him to comment with grave concern about 'overpopulation'. On the other hand, with a little more concern and a little less fear he would have realized that what disturbed him about the crowd in Dehli was not its numbers but its 'quality' – that is its poverty. To talk, as Ehrlich does, of 'overpopulation' is to say to people; you are poor because you are too many. [But] . . . people are not poor because they have large families. Quite the contrary: they have large families because they are poor. [M.Mamdani, 1972, pp.13-14.]

The 'quality' of a population coupled with the idea that what is best for the system is also in the best interests of the individuals involved, is the constant concern of controllers. Talk of 'quality' can involve thinly-disguised racism. It can be directed against the 'feckless' poor, and against marginal, 'problem' sections of the population. The line of causation is clear: overpopulation causes poverty and poverty causes unrest, remove the first factor and all the rest will fall in line. Thus Kingsley Davis, the renowned sociologist, explicitly outlines the political reasons for population control:

> The problem is not solely the swollen ranks of children. It is also the engorged contingents of youth. . . . Possessed of youthful energy and idealism, having no stake in the existing situation, being extremely numerous in relation to the adult population, these youths are politically explosive, often ready to follow the leader who promises the quickest and most violent solution. Their role in making and breaking dictators has often been demonstrated in backward countries, whether in Latin America or the Middle East. Their fiery impatience makes it hard for a ruler to follow a policy of basic economic development, for that seems too slow and too prosaic. It is easier for the ruler to satisfy the youthful rabble by threatening war, casting out the foreign devils, seizing property, and insulting the enemy – all in the name of sacred nationalistic sentiment and holy religious sentiment. [K.Davis, 1966, p.386.]

107

But it is not merely the young, for:

> The governments of non-industrial countries often harbour a well-founded suspicion of their growing urban masses. They know that city growth brings problems of frightening dimensions – problems of housing, sanitation, education, public order. They know that swollen city populations tend to become unruly and that they easily resort to riots and strife if the political leaders do not please them. The danger of urban mobs is all the greater in view of the fact that the city population are bulging with youth. [*ibid.* pp.389-390.]

Such anxiety reflects fear of the masses not only in the Third World but in the heartlands of capitalism itself. 'Urban crisis', we have noted, has been used to justify far-reaching reforms in the abortion-contraception field in the United States. In Britain, where delinquency and crime in the streets, although not yet of American proportions, are mounting, as are unemployment, urban dislocation and community breakdown, the more 'radical' wing of reformism is beginning to incline to Malthusian arguments. Thus Madeleine Simms writes:

> Against the perspective of our mounting concern with overpopulation, it is plainly nonsense to compel women to have babies they do not want to have, and who will, for this reason, be more expensive to bring up, and more likely than other children to be abused and do badly in later life. Any society that carries on its business in this way is irrational, in that its own policies are directed towards producing a state of affairs that weakens its own structure. [M.Simms, 'Abortion and liberation', 1972, p.5.]

Of necessity reformism takes progressive demands and pegs them to the needs of the system. Its role is to argue with the state that reforms are in the better interests of the system as a whole. In the abortion debate, although it can appear radical, it is riddled with the most insidious Malthusian and eugenic assumptions. Some of the effects on socialists can be seen in the following, doubtlessly well-intentioned, letter:

> What about the unwanted children that would be born if James White's Bill got passed? Madeleine Simms is right when she says . . . that women have not got a right to inflict the burden of handicapped

108

children on the state. Why should we overburden the state with unwanted people who take up so much of our resources?

We should now mobilize to get a truly socialist perspective on this issue. [J.Fielding, ALRA, *Women's Voice* no.23, 1975, p.8.]

Our concern, as socialists, is not to strengthen the state – and certainly we would not blanch as Ms Simms does, at the weakening of its structure. For it is not *our* state neither is it *our* resources. The right to choose must *not* be the right to help the ruling class out in terms of *their* population problems. Yet the reverse, the denial of all birth control measures as playing into the hands of the ruling class, is naive, however heartfelt. It is at this juncture that we can begin to tackle the problem formulated in the last chapter, namely how can birth control methods be utilized without their co-option into the population control programmes of the ruling class?

We have shown how in Britain the aims of the cautious brand of reformism which formed the spirit of the 1967 Act, were constantly diverted. For if the target population for abortion were to be the socially marginal, legislation would logically be restricted. Yet the women who were capable of exploiting the new legislation were precisely those who would be defined by reformers as 'normal', i.e. non-marginal. The only method of achieving their aims and reaching the less-educated, lower working class groups would have been to implement an unrestricted 'abortion on demand' system. But that, in turn, was ruled out because of the reformers' essentially conservative image of the social world and their consequent under-estimation of the 'real' need for abortion.

New York, in the throes of urban crisis, indicated clearly how a re-negotiated reformism could reach the social 'margins':

Table 5. Legal Abortions in US per 100 Live Births

	Population	White	Non-White
1951–53	New York City	0.41	0.14
1954–56	New York City	0.39	0.07
1957–59	New York City	0.38	0.06
1960–62	New York City	0.26	0.05
1969	Georgia married	0.12	0.04
1969	Georgia single	3.63	0.16
1970–71	New York residents	42.0	77.0
1971–72	New York residents	65.0	85.0 (est.)

Sources: B.Sarris and H.Rodman, 1973; C.Tietze, 1973, pp.36-41.

Prior to 1970 the legal abortion rate in that city was extremely small and there was a blatant inequality between white and non-white women. The inequality was growing: whereas in 1954 there was three times more chance of a white woman obtaining a legal abortion than a non-white, in 1962 it had risen to five times. Such inequality was to be found throughout the United States. In Georgia, for example, it was twenty-three times more likely for an unmarried white woman to obtain an abortion than her non-white counterpart.

In the early 1960s, 93 per cent of therapeutic abortions in New York were performed on white private patients; 42 per cent of pregnancy-related deaths resulted from illegal abortions; and one half of these women were black. [H.Pilpel, 1967.] Furthermore, the mortality rate from illegal abortions in New York City was higher amongst blacks than whites, in the order of four to one. [E.Gold and others, 1965, pp.964-972.]

After the 1970 Act the number of legal abortions not only expanded enormously, the ratio of black to white abortions reversed. Over time this difference increased so that the non-white

110

rate rose in two years from 77 to 85 per 100 live births and the percentage of non-white abortions on residents rose as follows:

Table 6. Abortions on New York Residents by Ethnic Group

	1970-71 %	1971-72 %
White	44.3	41.5
Puerto Rican	10.5	11.4
Non-White	45.2	47.1

Source: C.Tietze, 1973.

The non-white abortion rate is one of the highest in the world.

Table 7. International Comparison of Abortions per 100 Live Births

1973	Britain	17.0
1971	Sweden	17.1
1971	Czechoslovakia	39.8
1971	Bulgaria	98.5
1971	Hungary	122.8
1971–72	New York	
	Total	65.0
	Non-White (est.)	85.0

Figures such as these form the basis for Black Power accusations that the abortion campaign is genocidal, and for retorts, such as the black actor and comedian, Dick Gregory's: 'My answer to genocide, quite simply, is eight black kids – and another baby on the way.' [D.Gregory, 1971, pp.66-72.]

111

The New York legislation was an impressive step towards achieving the absolute right of women to regulate their own fertility because it involved no legal testing of eligibility for abortion up to twelve weeks of pregnancy. It enabled an immense number of working class women both black and white to free themselves from the predicament of having families too large for their incomes. It began the process of eliminating back street abortions and the inevitable toll of casualties that this involved. It was a woman's choice, a means for women to increase their potentiality for sexual, political and social equality. It was won through a struggle involving thousands of women, it changed their consciousness and ability to make choices independently.

These were the gains. What were the limitations?

Termination is available on request only where the woman is less than 24 weeks pregnant. Although the widespread availability and increasing acceptance of abortion considerably reduces the number who seek an abortion after 24 weeks, women still do not have full choice over their fertility.

An increasing number of abortions are performed in 'freestanding clinics', specialist units providing day release abortions by vacuum suction methods on women less than 12 weeks pregnant. The clinics have private arrangements with hospitals where the rare but serious complications can be effectively dealt with. Although a fair degree of public funding occurs through Medicare and a number of charities that work within the field, the clinics and other abortion facilities are all within the private sector. The price of an abortion in the clinics is $100 to $150 (1973), which is low by the standards of American private medicine. In cases of termination after 12 weeks, patients must attend a hospital where fees are considerably higher.

The law insists that the operation must be carried out by a licensed physician. This is where feminist groups make their major complaint. They insist that the new technique of menstrual extraction could eliminate the medical monopoly. Madeleine Simms described the innovation, in 1973, as:

112

a very simple suction device appropriate to the first week of suspected pregnancy, *before* pregnancy tests can be effective. It is therefore argued in some quarters that this ought not to be classified as an 'abortion' technique at all. The theologians and jurists are still fighting that one out. Meanwhile, a growing number of liberationists believe that this method is safe enough for women to be trained to use on each other, or even on themselves. No doctors, no clinics, no laws, no regulations, no money. The perfect method. [M.Simms, 'Abortion politics in New York', 1973, pp.252-253.]

The American women's movement has pointed out that since abortion is still a subject of legal control and the physician plays a crucial role in the process, reversal or re-direction of the present liberal legislation is always possible, particularly where powerful Catholic and conservative pressure groups exist. By developing the freestanding clinics using vacuum aspiration techniques and radically reducing the price, risk and traumatization of abortion medical interests acted, at first, in a progressive direction. But their financial and professional monopoly of the field has come to stand in the way of further progress. This is made worse by the fact that medicine in the United States is predominantly private.

The ultimate goal must be to stop treating abortion as a crime, which would entail removing all prohibitions on abortion and their replacement by laws governing any other surgical procedure. We also need to end the medical monopoly. This implies the development of techniques which would allow for lay practice and the use of para-medical staff.

It does *not* imply a situation where the state has no responsibility. It does not imply a reduction in standards for which some American feminists would seem to argue, as in the following statement:

At present the menstrual extraction method costs $30. If the city health regulations are strictly enforced, it is estimated that costs will rise to $100 . . . (the medical profession are) deaf to the clear evidence that there is a relation between quality of care and its cost. If a service includes every last refinement, it may be of the highest quality but only a few women may be able to afford it. [Ellen Frankfurt, in M.Simms, *ibid.* p.253.]

The right to abortion is a demand made of the state. This should mean the best possible medical facilities with the state under-writing the total cost. We must transform what was deemed a crime by the state to a legal right of the same order as Family Allowances and Social Security. To de-criminalize is not to abolish standards or to commit women to the cut-price medical shark. To destroy the medical monopoly is not to return to the back street amateur. It is to state that advances in techniques have made it possible for the vast majority of abortions to be accomplished by simple surgical procedures. These could well be performed by lay operatives given a short period of training and appropriate professional back-up facilities.

Feminist self-help groups in the abortion field should see themselves as ginger groups, akin to the pioneering schools of A.S.Neill and David Wills – standing as a critical exemplar of the state's interests and liabilities, not as replacements or alternatives.

The most fundamental criticism of the New York legislation is the accusation of black genocide. A black woman, Maxine Williams, succinctly dismisses such arguments:

If there should be a charge of 'genocide', it is the anti-abortion laws that must be condemned for causing the deaths of thousands of Black women across the country . . .

Far from being an attempt at genocide, the Supreme Court ruling will give Black women the right to control our bodies, thus allowing us to plan our lives with greater freedom. It will free us from unwanted pregnancies and save thousands of Black women from the hands of butcher abortionists.

To maintain therefore that Black women should not have control over our own bodies because we must produce more babies is to degrade women to the role of breeders. It is to say that Black women have no other function in the struggle except to produce offspring.

. . . the concept of babies for the revolution simply diverts the Black struggle. The degree to which our struggle advances depends primarily on the revolutionary consciousness of Black people and our ability to organise our people into action.

114

The women's liberation movement has rejected the argument that social problems will be solved by 'zero population growth'. Hunger and poverty are caused by an economic system that produces for profit, not by 'overpopulation'. The myth of 'too many babies' has simply been used to blame the poor, especially Black people, instead of the capitalist system, for the problems of society.

Legalizing abortion will not solve all our problems. But it is an important gain because it will place Black women in a better position to fight around other issues. Our struggles can only grow and expand because of the abortion victory. [M.Williams, 1973, p.10.]

The poverty of the ghetto drove many black women to illegal abortions. It killed black people just as lack of medical facilities, malnutrition and hardship shorten the lives of others. It is true that population controllers, especially those on the right, see liberal abortion legislation as a step towards reducing the black population and their cost to the social services. But because a piece of legislation is considered by the ruling class to be in their interests does not imply that there are no real advantages to be gained from it by the working class. Better ventilation may be justified by management as a way of increasing productivity, but this does not mean that it is not a gain for the workers. For the improvement in conditions can be extended even where no increase in productivity is forthcoming. Successful action on the part of workers is valuable beyond its immediate results because it generates the consciousness to press further demands against capital. The women's fight to achieve abortion as a right was phrased in absolute terms; it cut across the marginal concessions that population controllers were prepared to tolerate. This is the fulcrum of their achievement:

A turning point in the fight for the right to abortion came with the rise of women's liberation consciousness. Before the emergence of the new wave of feminism, supporters of legal abortion tended to present their arguments in a half-apologetic or wrong fashion – justifying it in terms of population control, or demanding legal abortion only in the case of birth defects, danger to the mother's life, rape, or incest. The women's liberation forces helped to pose the issue in a new way by stating categorically that abortion is a woman's right. The feminists took the issue off the axis of population control and placed it where it belonged – on the woman's right

115

to control her own body and her own life. [Linda Jenness, in L. Jenness and others, p.13.]

Neo-Malthusianism has been opposed from its very inception by socialists. It is hardly surprising. An editorial in the *Black Dwarf* suggested in 1823 that it was the population of drones, who ate without working, which ought to be checked rather than that of the working bees. But anti-Malthusianism on the left did not stem the use of contraceptives by the working classes. You did not have to believe with the neo-Malthusians that the world could be transformed by population control to realize that your own predicament could be rendered a little more manageable by effective forms of birth control. For contraceptives and abortion corresponded to a real need, however distorted and enmeshed it was in Malthusian opinion.

And why not? For if anti-Malthusianism is right in affirming that population control is not a panacea, birth control is scarcely a hindrance to the realization of socialism. No revolution was gained merely by weight of numbers, it is organization and consciousness which matter. Talk of numbers and genocide are by the way. Neo-Malthusianism is insidious at an ideological level, and underscores the necessity for socialists to link demands for fertility control to the wider context of social demands.

Even where the left conceded that birth control was important it tended to stop short of a feminist analysis, and to argue simply that women would be more effectively equal in the political struggle if they did not need to worry about unwanted children. However true this is, it is scarcely sufficient.

It was left to a few outstanding individuals, such as Robert Dale Owen and F.W.Stella Browne, to break through the barriers of male-dominated thinking and sexual prudery, and to argue that birth control was a necessity for the sexual liberation of women. It is this mantle that the modern women's movement has inherited and it is this position that needs constantly to be defended.

116

9.
The Control of Morality

> The preponderance of Labour members among the reformers high-
> lights an interesting paradox. The party which believes most in
> controlling economic behaviour and appetites is the same party
> which believes most in freeing the private sexual behaviour. Con-
> servatives on the other hand believe that the State should provide
> moral constraints but economic freedom. [K.Hindell and M.Simms,
> 1971, p.202.]

This passage, from Hindell and Simms, two of the most
prominent progressive reformers suggests that the Labour Party's
programme in economic issues is unrelated to their attitudes to
more 'private' matters. Such a belief is reinforced by the fashion in
which members of parliament are permitted a free vote on such
moral questions. But appearances are deceptive. The Labour
Party's reformism in industrial issues is of a piece with their reformism in other areas of life.

Both stem from the same world view – the idea that the
social order can be adjusted piecemeal, that social progress can be
achieved without fundamentally changing the social order and
that all 'rational' men and women can see the essentially just
nature of the social contract between public and parliament. The
large, durable problems are seen not as central to capitalism but
as occurring at the edges of the just society, in the marginal reaches
where irrationality and corruption abound.

Two images recur continuously in their analysis of social
problems whether it is industrial conflict, mugging or abortion –
the weak and the corrupter. While the normal, rational majority
sense the justice of the system and act accordingly, at the fringes

the constitutionally weak act irrationally because of their nature. Mental illness, violence, sexual 'aberrations', do not stem from a rotten society, but from the physiological and psychological compulsion of a tiny minority. And if widespread, *large-scale* deviations from the ruling norm occur, it is because of these weak elements in the population who are more at risk from outside influences than others. The weakness itself is imputed to innocence if the problem involves young people, or to ignorance if it involves women or the working class. Corrupt outside agencies play on this population: agitators fool the working class into engaging in strikes, machiavellian doctors persuade otherwise normal girls that they should have abortions. Thus the population is divided into four categories: the sick, who cannot help acting in a deviant way; the weak, who are corrupted into violating 'accepted' standards; the corrupters, who are either advocates of alien philosophies or in it for mercenary reasons; and the rational normal person, who realizes the sanity of the existing system. Nobody *chooses*, therefore, to violate bourgeois standards, their actions are either a product of their own personal inadequacy or of outside corrupting agents.

This is an ideology of the first order, and its insidiousness is further compounded by the way it inverts the causality of social problems. Strikes do not occur because of the class conflict endemic in capitalist society, rather they are a major *cause* of problems in capitalist society; mental illness is not a product of the stresses of the nuclear family and the wider society rather it is a *cause* of problems for the family and the social order.

Conventional images of abortion fit well into this picture. The inadequate woman is to be allowed abortion because of her essential fecklessness. The normal woman would not consider abortion unless for frivolous reasons spurred on by the advice of unscrupulous members of the medical profession.

But abortion is a special problem. It involves two components. It is a means of population control, and it also involves decisions about the nature of the family and sexuality. As far as

118

population control is concerned abortion can either be restricted in order to encourage the size of the population or be made more liberal in an attempt to reduce the birth rate. In practice, it is not a very sensitive regulator of the labour market, particularly when compared with migration. Immigrants can be shipped in very quickly, granted second class status in terms of citizenship, political rights, wages and demands on the social services, and deported again if changes in the labour market render them superfluous.

But if contraception and abortion are an imprecise and remote method for regulating employment they are seen as highly effective means of limiting the cost to the social services of lower working class groups. It is, therefore, in the interests of reformists to direct their abortion policy to this group. Ideologically this is easy as their map of the social order would label the marginal working class as inadequates and, therefore, precisely the group to whom abortion should be made available. Reformist legislation, therefore, reflects the ruling class *material* interests and is phrased in terms of reformist *ideas* as to the nature of the society.

Since only abortion on demand would fully cater for this 'marginal' population, and since 'normal' women seek abortion as soon as it becomes freely available, which suggests that there are not sufficient resources to let women throughout society have the children they desire, the reformists are in a difficult dilemma. Their practical economic concern to restrict certain sections of the population contradicts the central image of a society which can deliver the material goods.

But it is not only in the economic sphere that a conflict between practical concerns and ideology occurs. There is a problem in the second component of the reformist attitude to abortion, its relationship to sexuality and the family.

The nuclear family is seen as the most rational form of sexuality in society. Sexual pleasure is legitimate only if related to having children. Birth control is a threat in that it makes possible the split between sexuality and procreation.

Population control with its concern for rationalizing the

labour market and the social mix has persistently conflicted with *birth* control with its threat to the sanctity of the nuclear family. Their long fight over contraception was resolved by the concept of family planning. Just as the economy is planned so should the family be. Freedom from unwanted pregnancy is seen to fit with the maintenance of a stable family structure. Contraception should be available – to plan families. Mistakes occur of course. But that the 'normal' married woman existing in a family structure, which has as its raison d'être the bringing up of children, should resort to what is seen as the extreme measure of abortion, is untenable.

For abortion implies either that women do not instinctively welcome children or that the economic pressures on even the 'normal' family are such that an added child would present an insufferable burden, which poses considerable problems for the reformist world view. So when such women do seek abortion, reformists either argue that these apparently normal women are abnormal after all, or, following the general lines of their theory, that their action is the result of the influence exerted by corrupt members of the medical profession.

We have argued that the only way reformists can achieve their population control policy is through re-negotiating their conception of the social order. They have to see urban problems as being critical and involving a large proportion of the population. In such circumstances abortion on demand could be justified in their terms, as happened in 1970 in New York State. The justification will be distorted, seen in terms of overpopulation, crime in the streets, inevitable unemployment because of a mysterious recession of world markets. It will depict what are in reality the effects of capitalism as the causes of its problems, and will cast these factors as independent of the nature of the system. But that is to be expected. Material interests and ideas constantly interplay in abortion legislation, and incorrect ideas must constantly be readjusted to achieve a greater symmetry with material interests. Debates occur which take on the appearance of a confrontation between conservative and progressive tendencies. But however bitter, they are underpinned by the same reformist premises and represent attempts by reformists to renegotiate their definitions of a recalcitrant situation.

We have explained the practical concerns of reformist politics in the area of abortion and noted how the reformists' ideas about society can be renegotiated to fit their material interests. What remains unexplained is why such politics are supported by large sections of the population. After all it is in the interests of the working class and women as a whole that abortion should be freely available. Yet many find the idea abhorrent, and provide a massive if passive backing for reformist policies. The question is posed particularly sharply when even the timid changes brought about by the reformists are opposed by large groups within the country.

The existing social order with its mindless work tedium, its relentless restriction of individual potentiality and its incessant exploitation, rests on its ability to convince its members that its institutions are rational and embody just rewards. The control of work discipline and of sexuality is achieved to the extent that economic and sexual rewards are doled out according to commitment to the system. On the other side of the coin, failure, slackness, evasion of the rules must be punished, and be seen to be punished, for a lifetime of sacrifices at work and in the family must be seen to be justified – to make sense. Such a world view is bolstered by the idea that there is no alternative, by the appearance of the social world as beyond the power of people to change.

Yet cracks remain in the institutional shell; doubts stemming from the daily grind of the workplace and the suffocating routine of the family constantly threaten to overturn simple acquiescence. One response is to grasp the revolutionary alternative, to realize that it is possible to change the social order. Another response is to reaffirm the conventional virtues and to lash out at those who break the rules. Petty criminals, squatters, strikers, hooligans, social security recipients, the sexually promiscuous – all become scapegoats for moral anguish. A real anger about lack of housing devolves upon squatters and blacks. A genuine rage about just reward for work is projected on to social security recipients. A sad dismay at sexual repression is directed at those who break the established rules of sexual relationships.

Because of lack of organization and consciousness certain sections of the working class are particularly prone to such re-affirmation of conventional values when faced with threats to their income and status. But it is not only workers who respond in this way. The emergence of fascism in Germany related closely to the threatened lifestyle and privileges of the petit bourgeoisie; the Prohibition Movement in the United States represented a last stand by the small farmers of the Middle West against the encroachment of the urban, immigrant working class who threatened the tradi-tional virtues of thrift, puritanism and abstinence. [See J.R.Gus-field, 1963.]

In Britain certain sections of the lower middle class are similarly threatened. The income, job mobility and life-chances of the lower professionals (e.g. teachers, librarians, laboratory assis-tants) and of clerical workers have deteriorated so as to take them out of the margins of the managerial and higher professional groups and place them on the fringes of the manual working class. The median income of lower professionals has fallen to that of skilled workers and the wages of clerks are now below those of semi-skilled workers. [J.Westergaard and H.Resler, 1975, pp.73-76.]

For some of these occupational groups the relative decline has been accompanied by increased union militancy; but many are unorganized and defenceless. The trauma of inflation exacerbates further their plight. They cling to their status but without the in-come to back it.

It is people like these who form the backbone of a series of backward-looking organizations imbued with a notion of a golden age when traditional virtues were rewarded. The National Viewers and Listeners Association with Mary Whitehouse at its head, the Festival of Light, certain tendencies within the National Front, and the Society for the Protection of the Unborn Child – often with interlinking membership – represent, we believe, this stratum. At a time of crisis, such lower middle class groups react by reaffirming values which have long ceased to have any viability. How does abortion fit into these values whose enfeeblement is such a powerful source of moral indignation?

Pleasure must be harnessed to responsibility. Sexuality is legitimate only in relation to procreation in the nuclear family. The most satisfying and fruitful way of relating together sexually is in a family setting.

This equation of sexual happiness with procreation must have also its negative, namely, the belief that sexual practices outside the family are indulged in by the irrational and the feckless, and lead inevitably to unhappiness. But belief alone is insufficient to placate the morally indignant; their reactions serve to make the belief come true, to ensure that the wrongdoers suffer. The suffering is then seen as if it were part of a natural law of social intercourse, not a consequence of their own action; a fact of human nature not a human product.

The idea of coming to a bad end recurs in all areas of illicit pleasure. It is the Rake's Progress of ideology. It affirmed that marihuana use escalates to heroin addiction in the 1960s; that extra-marital intercourse results in VD – in the early twentieth century; that alcohol consumption leads to madness and dissipation – the Prohibition movement in the United States; that masturbation gives rise to insanity and impotence – late nineteenth century; that illegitimacy leads to personal catastrophe – nineteenth and early twentieth centuries.

These adages are often backed successfully by correlations produced by experts. What is forgotten is that such linkages are often a product of social stigmatization not an inherent facet of the activity, that measures can be taken to change such correlations, that they need not be regarded as absolute and law-governed.

However, anything that threatens to remove such inbuilt punishment mechanisms is opposed tooth and nail. As Alex Comfort writes of the medical profession's role in regulating sexual conduct:

[the anxiety maker] aims to make us frightened for our own good, whether he threatens us with hell-fire, particularly judgement, or disease. The other side of the coin to such propaganda is hostility, among the anxious, to factors in society which reduce the emotional tension – and particularly to those which give us increased freedom of choice. The campaign against these has occupied, and still occupies, sections of the Church and the medical and counselling professions. Just as the creation of anxiety over the sexual act and its moral and physical perils has been an important activity in our culture, so has resistance to anything which tended to reduce these perils.

Since the sixteenth century, when syphilis appeared in Europe, there were two major physical allies of conventional sexual anxiety – the spirochaete and the spermatozoon. Venereal disease might well have been invented by the anxious to prove their point . . . Here was a hazard of sex which could bring death, humiliation, insanity and disfigurement. Short of making the unmarried vagina radioactive, the Christian moralists . . . could not have hoped for a bigger bonanza than the pandemic spread of syphilis – all the most damaging guilt-feelings of the culture were actualized in it . . .

The second ally of God was, of course, illegitimate – and even legitimate – pregnancy. Atonement in the dangers of childbirth had been built into Eve's sexual life, and her frailer descendants could not with any hope of success attribute their extramarital conceptions to parthenogenesis. At the same time – since sex must obviously be tolerated for procreative purposes . . . potential fertility became a shibboleth: it made sexual activity a duty which could be distinguished from pleasure.

For these reasons attempts to prevent rather than control venereal disease, and to separate coitus from the risk of fertility, were deeply disturbing to anxiety makers. They still are. [A.Comfort, 1967, pp.136-137.]

Improvements in the control of venereal disease tended to occur only when the physical health of armies was in danger. And the battle for contraception could only be successful when the contradiction between its liberative sexual potential and the prevailing social order was resolved in the concept of family planning. For contraceptive measures removed the threat from free sexuality and it was only when their use was firmly embedded in the maintenance of the family that they could be tolerated.

The history of the struggle for contraception in Britain parallels that for abortion. At first advice was restricted to married women for whom pregnancy was a danger to health (1930) until eventually free contraceptive clinics were set up under the NHS Family Planning Act (1967).

A seeming quirk in the parallel is that contraceptive advice was allowed least readily to the unmarried whereas abortion facilities are, in intention at least, focused on them and frowned upon in relation to the majority of married women. This anomaly can be explained in terms of maintaining the link between procreation and sexuality. For children and sexuality are the province of the nuclear family. The married woman is within such a structure, sex is legitimate for her, and contraception aids family planning. The unmarried woman, on the other hand, would only be encouraged in her extra-familial sexuality by contraception. Abortion is the reverse of this, because the raison d'être of the nuclear family is children. Abortion is seen as permissible only to those women who are either outside of the family, or whose family would be threatened by it. The 'normal' married woman, in these terms, would be engaging in a senseless activity if she desired an abortion whilst in a procreative setting.

We have argued that the practical concerns of government underlie the reformers' policy over abortion. Sometimes their view of a just society in which work and sexuality are fulfilled is contradicted by what they see as the immediate economic interest. At such times of crisis they are able to revise their view of society sufficiently to extend abortion facilities. At such times they meet opposition which comes from those in society whose position is in decline, who have nothing to defend but a tradition of virtue threatened by an increasingly confusing society.

The struggle for abortion on demand is fought on a plane of moral premises and anxieties. SPUC supporters are anxious that the 'natural order' should remain, that intransigence should result

125

in the triumph of responsibility. The reformists wish to redefine abortion as planning for the feckless. Neither side dreams of liberation.

10.
The Right to Choose

What does the phrase the 'right to choose abortion' imply? It cannot be seen in isolation from the social possibilities available to women. A legal freedom means little if the social and political structures necessary to make it possible are absent.

The right to work, for example, is a just demand. But it does not represent freedom, far from it: its achievement within the present social setup implies the continued tyranny of exploited labour. It is necessary for sustenance and survival, no more than that. In a similar way, the right to abortion is necessary to give women a modicum of manoeuverability, but it is merely a right to make a choice amongst insufferable alternatives.

On the most elementary level the right to abortion is meaningful only if there are adequate facilities available for abortion and these are free. Without such resources it is merely a right of the rich to choose. It is only where resources are made available to minimize mortality and morbidity, to allow for early termination and to remove cost that such a freedom becomes a clearer choice for the mass of women. But however important it may be to demand abortion as a right, this choice is merely a freedom in a situation of strictly limited alternatives.

Abortion out of economic necessity is a tragedy. It must be demanded from government not as a dispensation to women but as a consequence of the government's own failure to provide facilities for children and support for the mother. Abortion out of choice, where no overriding economic pressures occur, is a fundamental right of women to control their own fertility, it is a comment on the inadequacy of contraceptive technology and it is a pre-requisite for women's social equality.

For the vast majority of women, whether middle class or working class, economic and social pressures severely constrain the choice. Circumstances dominate the decision not only for the working class woman whose husband might be on the dole; but also, if less obviously, for the professional woman whose choice is between a child and her job. She may actually experience her decisions as freedom, being unable to imagine that such a cross-road is anything other than a regrettable fact of life, not a social product that could be prevented.

Contraception and abortion together allow a woman to become political in that it is the *basis* for her equal participation in the politics both of sexuality and of the wider world. The tyranny of biological destiny need no longer dominate her to the extent that it has in all past historical periods.

But for this choice to be real it must occur in a society where alternatives are possible. On one side, physical facilities and emotional support must be available so that childbirth is not an overwhelming burden on a woman. On the other, fulfilling work must be available which provides a tenable alternative to child-rearing. This is not to pose work and child-rearing as necessary alternatives. Rather it is to argue that these two paths even if chosen separately do not exist for most women.

Viable childrearing and job alternatives alone do not provide an adequate basis for choice. Consciousness as well as material possibilities must change. Women's definition of themselves as only mothers is a product of history. It is a powerful definition, rooted in the social necessity of women to have children. And its obverse – women as inadequate – is a deeply felt and powerful emotion deeply rooted in existing sexual relationships.

The severance of procreation and sexuality threatens the age-old dependence of women on men. Pregnancy is often a weapon of control of women by men and of men by women. It can be used to confirm male dominance, it can shackle relationships which otherwise might naturally drift apart.

Choice can exist only to the extent that material alternatives exist and women are able to stand apart both from the restrictive definitions imposed by men and by the wider society. The women's movement facilitates such necessary changes in consciousness. It is in the struggle for better material conditions that the awareness of the possibilities of the new woman can take place.

A central argument of this book is that the struggle for a woman's right to control her own fertility is constantly in danger of being co-opted by the state. Legislation even when it embodies progressively increasing concessions is categorized and implemented in such a fashion as to suit ruling class interests.

The distinction between birth control and population control is paramount here. The first refers to the demands of women to decide whether or not to have children and involves a radical break between their procreative ability and their sexuality. The second, concerns the tactics of governments and their agencies to engineer the size and balance of their population in accordance with their economic interests. The first is a liberative achievement, the second smacks of a Malthusian disregard for the transformation of the social order, and for the possibility of doing so.

The task of socialist organizations is to make political demands in this field which constantly separate the two poles of this debate. This does not imply making utopian demands which are so far ahead of the mass movement as to gain little political support, or being blithely unaware of the political possibilities in a given country at a given time. On the contrary, genuine choice can only emerge out of the rising consciousness of women in struggle, and our tactics must constantly take cognizance of the political terrain in which we are working. The demands in a predominantly Roman Catholic country with extremely restrictive abortion laws would differ from those where legislation is permissive. Similarly, we should be aware of the inherent contradictions of the reformist position in order to understand which concessions are possible, and which arguments can best take advantage of their intellectual confusion.

In the following list we have concentrated on demands appropriate to Britain, at this present period:

1. Abortion as a real choice

To promote a genuine choice, especially amongst working class women, demands for abortion must go hand in hand with those which will facilitate child-rearing. This involves state provision of nurseries and play-groups, sufficient minimum incomes, satisfactory family allowances, and more adequate housing. Where abortion occurs because of economic necessity, it is essential to stress that we are not demanding abortion as a right granted to women by a kind parliament but as a duty of the state towards its citizens which arose *because* of its failure to provide the requisite facilities for child-rearing. Abortion must not be presented as a negative campaign. As Halpern, Kenrick and Young put it:

> the right to choose still has to be fought for. At this point in time we can get contraceptives, abortions, etc. on the National Health Service but provision is inadequate and we cannot rely on those services always to be provided and not to be used against us. Thus we must do all that is necessary both to fight for an extension of existing facilities and to ensure that we may still be able to choose if it becomes state policy to reduce or increase the birth rate. One such line of action is to find out more about how our bodies work and to disseminate this knowledge.

> The right to choose is often seen only as a right to refuse to have children. The right must also include that of having children. We must always defend women against the criticism of having 'too many' children.

> Then, since one's choice depends very largely on economic factors, especially the provision of housing, schools and medical services, decent creches, etc, we must constantly emphasize that the decision to have children is not – as the population lobby would imply – a question of tailoring family size to *existing* social provisions. [P.Halpern and others, 1974, p.168.]

In this fashion, the demand discriminates effectively between population control and birth control. Population control bestows

130

its favours upon a depressed section of the community: it sees abortion as a palliative. Birth control responds to the demands of *all* women for a reasonable life. It never forgets that the social circumstances which have resulted in limited choice come from a system unwilling and unable to manage its affairs in the interests of the bulk of the population. Population control bestows, birth control demands.

2. Abortion as a universal demand

Reformers will admit to there being problems – but only at the margins of society. In contrast we must reject all legal distinctions between permissible and illicit abortion, whether it is in terms of the social background of the woman, her age, or the length of pregnancy. Abortion is a woman's right, it is a necessity for women across a wide spectrum of social circumstances whether because of their economic situation, their emotional predicament or because of a plain desire to terminate her pregnancy. Ending a situation where abortion is a criminal offence is crucial. For doctors and judges to interfere in the woman's decision is an impertinence. If this can be achieved, the aims of population control will be defeated – the *woman* not the expert élite will make the choice.

But we must distinguish long-term aims and strategic demands. In the present political context to fight for abortion on demand up to twenty-four weeks (ALRA's present proposals) has the virtue of being a realizable achievement. It would cater for the vast majority of cases – only 200 abortions were performed after twenty-four weeks in 1974 – and the improvement in availability would further cut into the minority. Although the figures are not to be taken at face value since many requests are turned down in the period, and many more never made for fear of refusal, abortion on demand up to twenty-four weeks could well create a situation where abortion on demand without a time limitation effectively existed – so it would then be relatively easy to call for legal acceptance of the situation. With such a victory behind it, the campaign should then turn its focus towards total abortion on demand.

It is important to see abortion on demand up to twenty-four weeks as a strategic demand and *not* as part of an argument centering on the viability of the foetus. To do the latter is to accept the division of abortion into two legal categories : the permissible and the abhorrent. This is not de-criminalization. It would place abortion as a special medical category involving unique decisions on the preservation of life, decisions which are, in fact, a commonplace of medical practice. Furthermore, to accept arguments about foetal viability is to render oneself constantly vulnerable to medical advances providing progressively earlier viability and increasingly restricting a woman's right to choose.

3. Abortion is a demand on the state

Abortion is a right of the individual and the provision of facilities a duty of the state in so far as the necessity for abortion is often a product of precisely the social order which the state safeguards. Furthermore, to the extent that the bourgeois state pretends to further the equality and liberty of its citizens, the onus is on it to ensure the fundamental right of women to exist in a situation where their freedom and social equality is not constantly hampered by fears of unwanted pregnancy.

This involves the provision of the best medical facilities within the National Health Service. For feminist self-help groups to provide this service is courageous but it remains at best a ginger-group activity – it is not the role of radical groups to take over the duties of a state health service. The stage has now been reached for them to be integrated into the NHS, as happened previously with the Family Planning agencies. Just as the state is obliged to provide for childbirth, so should it be obliged to cater for all birth control and abortion facilities.

4. The breaking of the medical monopoly

To urge the de-criminalization of abortion is not to maintain that medical expertise is irrelevant. On the contrary, a surgical

132

operation of however minor a nature should rest on the best possible medical treatment. But doctors should be used as technicians not moral arbiters. Furthermore, a sufficiently permissive climate would make for early termination in the vast majority of cases and would therefore entail relatively minor surgery. In such conditions there is no reason for suitably trained para-medical staff not to be employed, particularly if the medical profession resist the deployment of their members into this work.

The most favourable setting for such an endeavour would be the day clinic with facilities for reference to specialized hospitals in cases involving any degree of complication.

5. The opposition to 'professional counselling'

The population controllers align themselves with the need for birth control through the paternalistic medical and social work counsellors. The bias of their intercession is towards coaxing marginal women into abortion and sterilization and dissuading 'normal' women. Unfortunately, so great is their prestige and authority and so sensitive and guilt-ridden many of the clients, that their advice can be very influential. It is necessary, therefore, to oppose any legislation which contains within it notions of compulsory counselling (as, for example, in Sweden – Abortion Amendment Bill, 1975) and to interpose between the state and the individual, counsellors whose sympathies lie with the women's movement. For an important counselling role exists at each stage in the process of having an abortion.

First, the real alternatives for the individual should be discussed: housing facilities, social security support, effect of childbirth on job opportunities and the possibility of day nurseries. At the same time, pressures from parents or the father of the child should be discussed, and a candid assessment of the amount of concrete support they would give if the woman were to have the child.

Second, if abortion is chosen, the essential minor and 'normal' nature of the operation should be pointed out in order to

133

remove feelings of guilt. Women who have had abortions themselves would be useful counsellors here.

Third, alternative abortion techniques and the facilities available should be deliberated together with a description of what happens during the operation. Finally, post-abortion counselling can eliminate unnecessary trauma and suggest suitable contraceptive measures to be used in the future.

6. Demand for research

> An adequate abortion law would also encourage *constructive* research. There is no reason to suppose we are at more than the mere alphabet of chemistry and psycho-biology in this matter . . . the invention and circulation of a perfectly reliable and otherwise tolerable abortifacient – especially if it could be self-administered – would be the greatest gift science could give to women. This triumph is perhaps possible within measurable time – unless indeed such civilisation as Europe has achieved should pass away under a deluge of the high explosives and poison gases which afford so lucrative and respectable a branch of research and industry. The right to abortion is a keypoint going deep down to the roots of social philosophy and economic reality. [F.W.Stella Browne, 1935, pp.33-34.]

F.W.Stella Browne's plea for a science directed towards the people still stands today despite massive advances in birth control techniques. A whole series of physical and chemical devices have been developed but the suspicion is growing that the needs being catered for are those of the pharmaceutical companies and population control agencies rather than the aesthetic, emotional, sexual and health interests of individual women. Emphasis is on *cost* rather than needs and preferences. As Carol Dix put it :

> It is well over ten years since the euphoria that greeted the new wonder-drug, the Pill, and it is about now that, after much shopping around, a lot of women have had to face the alarming truth – not only is there no magic contraceptive but they may have been persuaded to use harmful techniques, believing that contraceptives are good for them because they are good for society. Has a figurative woollen cap been pulled over our eyes and have we, like women from Third World countries been treated like potential breeders who must be stopped? [C.Dix, *Guardian*, 6 November 1974, p.9.]

134

Dix interviewed a series of women whose experience with IUDs and the Pill were horrific in the extreme. She quotes Robert Snowden, director of Exeter University's family planning project:

> If we're being honest every single method of fertility regulation is unpleasing. So what choice women make out of unpleasing ones is interesting. We want to see, too, whether the providers look on their service as population control or a service for a better quality of life. From there . . . we can investigate what kind of device to try and make. Maybe we could develop ones that would improve our sex lives! [*ibid.* p.9.]

Technology alone does not create liberation. It just provides the possibilities. What is needed is a society which will throw its resources into creating such a technology.

As a result of liberalizing legislation and because of the ginger group activities of the women's movement progress has occurred in abortion techniques. Vacuum aspiration techniques, which are extremely safe in the first three months of pregnancy and dispense with a general anaesthetic and admission to hospital, were developed in Eastern Europe where abortion is liberal by current standards. In the West too, the achievement of liberal legislation allowed far more open research and the development of techniques with a focus on earlier, and thus safer, termination. In Britain, as we have shown, this created the technical arguments for even greater liberalization.

Technological research to separate sexuality from procreation and to reduce sexual anxieties should focus on four chief areas. The development of efficient and aesthetic contraceptive devices. The curtailment of venereal disease. The provision of techniques and facilities for the prompt assessment of pregnancy. The achievement of extremely early abortion where necessary. This last project would do much to remove trauma, reduce further risks of illness and death, and deflate the arguments on foetal rights.

7. The need for a mass movement

We might be accused of being harsh on the Abortion Law

Reform Association and of under-estimating their role in reform. If we have under-played their achievements it is because the current struggle has been undermined by their limitations.

The élitism characteristic of conventional pressure group politics blinded ALRA to the necessity of a mass-based movement the building of which might have resulted in the achievement of more thoroughgoing results at an earlier date. But leading members of ALRA denied its possibility :

> The abortion law reform campaign was not a mass campaign though it would have been had all the women who had ever sought abortion joined it. English social reforms never are, whatever the pretensions of their supporters. Neither the abolition of capital punishment, nor prison reform, nor divorce law reform, nor homosexual law reform was pushed through by public clamour. [K.Hindell and M.Simms, p.242.]

The reforms they mention gather little wide-scale support precisely because they are directed towards marginal groups. But abortion law reform affects the vast majority of women. The result was that ALRA's limited perspectives gave ammunition to the anti-abortionists and ALRA could not fully understand what happened after the Abortion Act of 1967.

Turning the campaign into a mass movement in the interests of the majority of society would have strengthened ALRA – and broadened the argument. Women's freedom, the conditions needed to bring up children, and the separation of procreation from sexuality matter to *everybody*. They are the real arguments against the population controllers.

ALRA's younger members with roots in the women's movement have transformed the organization. It is they who, with other groups, started a mass movement through the Working Women's Charter Campaign. They remain, however, a pressure group working within the umbrella organization, NAC.

A problem remains – how to weld the short-term concerns of ALRA with the total demands of NAC. There is a risk of slipping back into pressure group politics or, alternatively, of drifting into utopianism.

8. The place of a one-issue campaign

To view a woman's right to choose as relevant only when there are real alternatives and as part of a struggle to achieve real freedom is to adopt a position which does not focus on a *single* issue. Free abortion on demand might be wrung out of the existing powers but it will be a limited and temporary gain unless it involves the fundamental transformation of society.

Campaigns on single issues are useful only if linked to organizations which generalize the issue in the context of wider social demands. Otherwise, the mass involvement they generate evaporates with the topicality of the issue. Even when 'successful' they are liable to be co-opted and remain vulnerable to the depredations of reformism.

In present-day Britain the two most obvious sources of organizational support for the abortion campaign are the women's movement and the revolutionary left. But the women's movement is a heterogeneous collection of tendencies, some apolitical, some anti-socialist in their orientation. And the revolutionary left displays a bewildering sectarianism and a distinct bias towards viewing women's issues as marginal concerns, subsuming them simplistically into the rhetoric of class analysis, and of interest to the left chiefly as an easy recruiter to socialism.

A more coherent underpinning would be based on the Working Women's Charter. It presents a series of interim demands on the state as follows:

We pledge ourselves to agitate and organise to achieve the following aims:

MAIN DEMAND
1. For the right of women to work, jobs for all – security of employment for part-time and casual workers.
2. The rate for the job, regardless of sex or race, at rates negotiated by the trade unions. For a national minimum wage below which no wages should fall. For this national minimum wage and all benefits

and wages to be fully protected against inflation by automatic increases based on a working class cost of living index.

3. Equal opportunity of entry into occupations and in promotion, regardless of sex, age, race, marital status or sexual orientation.

4. Equal education. Training for all occupations and compulsory day release for 16-19 years olds in employment. Equal access to apprenticeships and positive discrimination in training for jobs where few women are presently employed.

5. Equality for women in working conditions and conditions of employment, without deterioration of previous conditions . . .

6. The removal of all legal and bureaucratic barriers to equality, regardless of sex, marital status and sexual orientation, with regards to tenancies, mortgages, pension schemes, taxation, passports, care, control and custody over children, social security payments, insurance and supplementary benefits, and hire purchase agreements.

7. Free state-financed, community controlled child care facilities . . . to be available for all under-fives. The integration of day care and educational facilities. The provision of play facilities after school and during the school holidays for all children.

8. A minimum of eighteen weeks paid pregnancy leave. Adequate paternity leave. The right for either parent to take a year's child care leave after birth, half of which to be paid. No dismissal during pregnancy, paternity or child care leave. No loss of security, pension or promotion prospects. Paid leave to care for sick children . . . for both men and women.

9. Birth control clinics to be extended to cover every locality. For free and safe abortion, contraception, vasectomy and sterilisation on demand on the NHS.

10. Child benefits to be increased to £5 per child . . . Benefits to be protected against inflation, and to be tax free and non deductible from social security, supplementary and insurance benefits.

11. To campaign amongst women to take an active part in trade unions and political life and to push for any structural and organisational changes needed to achieve this. To campaign amongst trade union men so that they too may work to achieve these aims.

[*Working Women's Charter*, April 1976 (to be ratified 1977.)]

Such a series of linked demands provides a basis for women to make a real choice whether to have a child or not, insisting as it does that contraception and abortion should be freely available on demand; that the mother should be able to choose to work or not without hardship; and that a real occupational and financial choice should exist. Such a charter serves as a common platform for individuals working in the women's movement and the various segments of the revolutionary left.

In such a fashion not only can the abortion debate be directly related to the limited alternatives facing women in practice in our society but can be widened in terms of general demands put forward from a socialist perspective. Restrictions on NHS facilities for abortion, for instance, can be related to the general opposition to private medicine and to cuts within the public sector. It is only if such a common platform is fought for within the broad labour movement that organizations like NAC can be maintained on a mass basis rather than degenerate into pressure groups with narrow horizons confined to parliamentary debate.

> They say no, no – no more kids; the welfare worker she tells you you're 'overpopulating' the world and something has to be done. But right now one of the few times I feel good is when I'm pregnant, and I can feel I'm getting somewhere, at least then I am – because I'm making something grow, and not seeing everything die around me, like all it does in this street, I'll tell you. They want to give me the pill and stop the kids, and I'm willing for the most part; but I wish I could take care of all the kids I could have, and then I'd want plenty of them. Or maybe I wouldn't. I wouldn't have to be pregnant to feel hope about things. I don't know; you can look at it both ways, I guess. [R.Coles cited in D.Callahan, 1970, p.505.]

Daniel Callahan commenting on these words of a black American woman astutely notes how the liberalization of abortion laws by themselves is a half-freedom. Reformism will sometimes allow a choice, but it is a choice to be made in a world where freedom is so severely circumscribed as to be often little choice at all. We must fight for this choice but make no bones about its limitations. Unless we place our demands within a wider perspective and fully realize the propensity of reformism to grant concessions of its own choosing, we can all to easily lose sight of the fundamental transformation of the society which is necessary if real freedom is to be possible.

Two goals determine our course. Firstly, the liberation of

human sexuality from the anxieties of unwanted childbirth; secondly, the restructuring of the social order so that procreation can be a genuine choice. The relations between men and women will change profoundly with their achievements. A fundamental transformation in the present society is necessary for their realization.

Postscript

On 28 July 1976 the Select Committee on Abortion published its *First Report*, (Volume 1) H.C. 573-1. Its membership had been depleted by the resignation of all six members sympathetic to the existing workings of the 1967 Act; the evidence it surveyed was biased since all the pro-abortionist organizations subsequently blacked the Committee. But, despite the anti-abortionist influences on the Committee, the *Report* represented a clear triumph for the middle-ground of opinion; that is, for the brand of conservative reformism which Leo Abse and James White represent. Abse has reaffirmed this position in his explanation of the ground rules of the Committee:

> merely to affirm the principle that every child – legitimate, illegitimate, disabled, black, whether born in a manger or palace – should be warmly received into our society can be only too often in our imperfect world, taunting rhetoric to a woman wracked by her predicament. Parliament, acknowledging with realism its defeat to provide a world, even in an affluent society, where no child need suffer lack of care, passed the Abortion Act in 1967. The sponsors of that Act insisted that its aim was not to provide abortion on demand: its declared objective was to ensure that in particular limited medical and social circumstances abortion would no longer be illegal in Britain.
>
> Unhappily, by ineptitude or guile, the Act was clumsily and loosely drafted. The Royal Assent was no sooner given than the predatory moved in and were able, with legal immunity, to exploit brutally the troubled woman hesitant in her pregnancy. [Leo Abse, 'Putting a stop to the abortion industry', *The Times*, 29 July 1976, p.14.]

We have argued throughout that the reformers constantly under-estimate the genuine demand for abortion and are forced to explain the abortion rate in terms of corruption by unscrupulous doctors. The recommendations of the *Report* bear out this view.

To start with the *Report* insists that the two doctors who authorize an abortion shall not be in private practice together or have financial links. Moreover, to ensure that the decision is taken by doctors 'with maturity and insight', it recommends that at least one of the certifying doctors should have been registered for a minimum of five years. This stipulation obviously hinges on the belief that the financial interests of doctors is a major factor in encouraging abortion. If implemented, it would clearly reduce the influence of younger GPs with more progressive beliefs.

The *Report* then turns to the advisory bureaux and the charitable clinics. All such bureaux, it insists, must be statutorily approved and severed from any financial links with the clinics. It also calls for their charitable status to be revoked. But the rise of the private sector to prominence in the first place was a direct result of the under-estimation of the potential demand for abortion and the unwillingness to provide adequate NHS facilities.

The *Report* further insists that the individual need no longer furnish proof of conscientious objection to performing abortions. Such a simplification of the grounds for exemption from abortion duties would reduce considerably the effective availability of abortions on the NHS.

The *Report* proposes that the upper limit for termination should be restricted, reducing it from the current limit of 28 weeks to 20 weeks (with the exception of those women whose children might be born with a major disability, or whose health would be seriously threatened). Two arguments are advanced. Firstly, that 'no civilized country allows, as this country does, abortion to take place up to 28 weeks' gestation' (Abse, *The Times*, 29 July 1976). Second, that advances in medical techniques have extended the period of foetal viability. In a 'civilized' country, of course, nearly all abortions would occur in a very early period because ample

142

abortion facilities would be readily available.

If the recommendations of the July 1976 *Report* were to be adopted, abortions would be more difficult to obtain. The process would take longer, yet the number of weeks available would be further restricted. The results would be a new black market in abortions and further hardship for the very women whom Abse and the reformers generally see as most needy. The irony of the reformers' position is that only abortion on demand will cater for this most exploited group of women.

29 July 1976.

Bibliography

Official documents

Parliamentary debates on abortion are to be found in Hansard under the following dates.

UK Parliamentary Debates, *Official Report* (Hansard): *House of Commons*.

    10 February 1961, vol.634
    15 June 1965, vol.714 col.661
    26 February 1966, vol.725 col.56
    22 July 1966, vol.732 col.60
    2 June 1967, vol.747 col.726
    30 June 1967, vol.749 col.222
    13 July 1967, vol.750 col.232
    25 October 1967, vol.751 col.734
    15 July 1969, vol.787 col.149
    7 February 1975, vol.885 col.63
    21 October 1975, vol.898 col.182
    4 December 1975, vol.901 col.12
    9 February 1976, vol.905 col.44

UK Parliamentary Debates, *Official Report* (Hansard): *House of Lords*.

    30 November 1965, vol.270
    1 February 1966, vol.272
    7 February 1966, vol.272
    22 February 1966, vol.273
    28 February 1966, vol.273

7 March 1966, vol.273
10 May 1966, vol.274
23 May 1966, vol.274
19 July 1967, vol.285
26 July 1967, vol.285
27 July 1967, vol.285
23 October 1967, vol.285
26 October 1967, vol.285

Reports of the House of Commons Select Committee on the Abortion (Amendment) Bill 1975:

H.C.253 (i) 14 April 1975
H.C.253 (ii) 21 April 1975
H.C.253 (iii) 28 April 1975
H.C.253 (iv) 5 May 1975
H.C.253 (v) 12 May 1975
H.C.253 (vi) 19 May 1975
H.C.253 (vii) 9 June 1975
H.C.253 (viii) 16 June 1975
H.C.253 (ix) 23 June 1975
H.C.253 (x) 20 June 1975
H.C.253 (xi) 7 July 1975
H.C.253 (xii) 20 October 1975
H.C.253 (xiii) 27 October 1975
H.C.253 (xiv) 3 November 1975

Select Committee on the Abortion (Amendment) Bill 1975, First Special Report, H.C.253, 3 March 1975.
"   Second Special Report, H.C.496, 21 July 1975.
"   Recommendations, H.C.552, 30 July 1975.
"   Fourth Special Report, H.C.692-i, 10 November 1975.

Abortion (Amendment) Bill 1975, (Bill 19) 47/1, 27 November 1974.

Report of the Lane Committee on the Working of the Abortion Act, vol.I Cmnd.5579, vol.2 Cmnd.5579-I, vol.3 Cmnd. 5579-II.

Books and pamphlets

Abortion Law Reform Association, 'The first year of the Act'. Mimeo.

"   'The first eighteen months of the Act'. Mimeo.

"   'The first two years'. Mimeo.

"   *A Guide to the Abortion Act 1967*, ALRA 1968.

"   *Evidence to Committee of Inquiry into the Working of the 1967 Abortion Act (1972)*, ALRA 1972.
Memorandum to the Select Committee on the Abortion (Amendment) Bill 1975, ALRA 1975.

"   *Why We Must Fight the Abortion (Amendment) Bill*, ALRA 1975.

"   *Action Guide*, ALRA 1975.

"   *How Much Choice?* ALRA 1975.

D.Baird, 'Social research and obstetric practice', *Question*, January 1969.

D.P.C.Beazley and J.Knight, 'To be or not to be? The pros and cons of abortion', Conservative Party Centre, no.562 1974. Leaflet.

M.Bone, *Family Planning Services in England and Wales*, HMSO 1973.

British Pregnancy Advisory Service, *Abortion Today: Facts, Figures and Comments, no.1*, 2nd ed. 1975.

F.W. Stella Browne and others, *Abortion*, 1935.

D.Callahan, *Abortion: Law, Choice and Morality*, Collier Macmillan 1970.

R.Coles, 'Who's to be Born?' *New Republic*, 10 June 1967.

A.Comfort, *The Anxiety Makers*, Nelson 1967.

Kingsley Davis, 'The world population crisis', in R.Merton and R.Nisbet (eds.), *Contemporary Social Problems*, 2nd ed. New York, Harcourt, Brace & World 1966.

P.Ehrlich, *The Population Bomb*, New York, Ballantine Books 1968.

P.Ferris, *The Nameless*, Hutchinson 1966.

146

J.M.Finnis, 'The Abortion Act: what has changed?', *Criminal Law Review*, January 1971.

E.Gold and others, 'Therapeutic abortions in New York City', *American Journal of Public Health*, no.55, 1965.

G.B.Goodhart, 'On the incidence of illegal abortion' with a reply to Dr W.H.James, *Population Studies*, vol.27 no.2, July 1973.

L.Gordon, 'The politics of population, birth control and eugenics', *Radical America*, vol.8 no.4, 1974.

V.Greenwood, 'Theft of the body: a sociology of the abortion law'. Unpublished MA thesis, University of Sheffield 1973.

D.Gregory, 'My answer to genocide', *Ebony*, October 1971.

J.R.Gusfield, *Symbolic Crusade*, University of Illinois Press 1963.

P.Halpern, J.Kenrick and K.Young, 'Some thoughts on a "woman's right to choose" ', in *Women and Socialism: Conference Paper 3*, Birmingham Women's Liberation Group, 1974.

G.Hardin, 'Abortion and human dignity', in A.F.Guttmacher (ed.), *The Case for Legalized Abortion Now*, Berkeley, Diablo Press 1967.

P.Harrison, 'Abortion: what the trends are', *New Society*, 31 July 1975.

K.Hindell and M.Simms, *Abortion Law Reformed*, Peter Owen 1971.

A.Hordern, *Legal Abortion: The English Experience*, Pergamon 1971.

International Marxist Group, 'Free abortion on demand', IMG, n.d. Leaflet.

International Planned Parenthood Federation, Europe Region, 'Legal abortion in Britain', 1973.

International Planned Parenthood Federation, Europe Region, 'Induced abortion and family health: a European view', 1973.

W.H.James, 'The incidence of illegal abortion', *Population Studies*, vol.25 no.2, July 1971.

L.Jenness, C.Lund and C.Jaquith, *Abortion: A Woman's Right*, New York, Pathfinder Press 1971.

L.Jenness, 'The Supreme Court ruling on abortion: how the victory was won', in L.Jenness and others, *Abortion: Women's Fight for the Right to Choose*, New York, Pathfinder Press 1973.

M.Kohl, *The Morality of Killing, Sanctity of Life, Abortion and Euthanasia*, Peter Owen 1974.

J.Lambert, 'Survey of 3,000 unwanted pregnancies', *British Medical Journal*, October 1971.

League for Socialist Action, 'Abortion: a woman's right', LSA 1975. Pamphlet.

T.L.T.Lewis, 'The Abortion Act', *British Medical Journal*, 25 January 1969.

M.Litchfield and S.Kentish, *Babies for Burning*, Serpentine Press 1974.

M.Mamdani, *The Myth of Population Control*, New York, Monthly Review Press 1972.

B.Mass, *The Political Economy of Population Control in Latin America*, Quebec, Éditions Latin-America 1972.

R.Meek, *Marx and Engels on Malthus*, Lawrence & Wishart 1953.

H.Pilpel, 'The abortion crisis', in A.Guttmacher (ed.), *The Case for Legalized Abortion Now*, Berkeley, Diablo Press 1967.

Pregnancy Advisory Service. *Report 1971-1973*, PAS 1974.

J.Rakusen, 'New pregnancy test', *Spare Rib* 41, November 1975.

S.Rowbotham, *Hidden from History*, Pluto Press 1973.

B.Sarris and H.Rodman, *The Abortion Controversy*, New York, Columbia University Press 1973.

J.J.Scarisbrick, 'What's wrong with abortion?', Leamington Spa, Life 1971. Pamphlet.

M.Simms, 'The great foetus mystery', *New Scientist*, 31 December 1970.

M.Simms, 'The Abortion Act: a reply', *Criminal Law Review*, February 1971.

148

M.Simms, 'The Abortion Act after three years', *Political Quarterly*, 42, July-September 1971.

M.Simms, 'Abortion and liberation', New York, Association for the Study of Abortion, 1972. ASA Reprint.

M.Simms and C.Ingham, 'Study of applicants for abortion', *Journal of Bio-Social Science*, 4, 1972.

M.Simms, 'Abortion politics in New York', *New Scientist*, 1 February 1973.

M.Simms, 'Five years after the Abortion Act', *New Scientist*, 8 November 1973.

M.Simms, 'Abortion law and medical freedom', *British Journal of Criminology*, April 1974.

M.Simms, 'Gynaecologists, contraception and abortion – from Birkett to Lane', *World Medicine*, no.23, October 1974.

M.Simms, 'The progress of the Abortion Amendment Bill', Parts 1 and 2, *Family Planning*, vol.24 nos. 2 and 3, 1975.

M.Simms, 'The compulsory pregnancy lobby – then and now', *Journal of the Royal College of General Practitioners*, no. 25, 1975.

M.Simms, 'Abortion since 1967', *New Humanist*, vol. 91 no. 10, 1976.

Society for the Protection of the Unborn Child (SPUC), 'Need we kill 450 every day?', n.d. leaflet.

T.Szasz, 'The ethics of abortion', *Humanist*, October 1966.

C.Tietze, 'Two years' experience with a liberal abortion law: its impact on fertility trends in New York City', *Family Planning Perspectives*, vol. 5 no.1, 1973.

C.Tietze and D.Dawson, 'Induced abortion: a fact book', New York, Population Council 1973. (Reports on Population/ Family Planning.)

C.Tietze and S.Lewit, 'Joint program for the study of abortion: early medical complications of legal abortion', *Studies in Family Planning*, June 1972.

D.F.Walbert and J.D.Butler, *Abortion, Society and the Law*, Cleveland Ohio, Western Reserve University Press 1973.

149

J.Westergaard and H.Resler, *Class in a Capitalist Society*, Heinemann 1975.

M.Whitehouse, *Cleaning up TV*, Blandford Press 1967.

D.Widgery, 'Abortion: the Pioneers', *International Socialism*, no. 80, July 1975.

Dr and Mrs J.C.Wilkie, 'Life or death', Society for the Protection of the Unborn Child (SPUC) 1972.

G.Williams, *The Sanctity of Life and the Criminal Law*, Faber 1958.

M.Williams, 'Abortion victory for black women', in L.Jenness and others, *Abortion: Women's Fight for the Right to Choose*, New York, Pathfinder Press 1973.

World Health Organization, 'Spontaneous and induced abortion', Geneva, WHO 1970. (Technical Report Series, no.461.)

World Health Organization, 'Induced abortion as a public health problem', Helsinki, WHO 1971.

N.Yoshiko, 'Women fight for control: abortion struggle in Japan', Tokyo 1973.

S.Young, 'The politics of abortion: women and the crisis in the National Health Service', *Radical Science Journal*, no.2/3, 1975.

Index

Sheila Rowbotham

Hidden From History:
300 years of women's oppression
and the fight against it

An account of the changing position of women in England from the Puritan revolution to the 1930s.

Hidden from History brings together a mass of material on birth control, abortion and female sexuality; on the complex relationship of women's oppression and class exploitation and on the attempts to fuse the struggles against the two.

Sheila Rowbotham concludes that real equality for women depends, and has always depended, on 'our capacity to relate to the working class and the action of working class women in transforming women's liberation according to their needs'.

Available from bookshops and
Pluto Press
Unit 10 Spencer Court, 7 Chalcot Road
London NW1 8LH

Werner Thönnessen

The Emancipation of Women:
The rise and decline of the women's movement in Germany 1863-1933

Nearly all the problems posed by women's liberation today were discussed politically in the German labour movement at the turn of the century.

Thönnessen's book – the first major study to appear in English – is a careful record of those discussions. It also records the non-solutions accepted at the time by socialist women.

Frank Pearce

Crimes of the Powerful:
Marxism, Crime and Deviance

In his critique of traditional criminology and the radical deviancy school, Frank Pearce lays the foundations for a marxist criminology – rooted in an analysis of the mode of production in society and the social relations between classes. He deploys this theoretical framework in two detailed studies – of 'corporate crime' and 'organized crime' – both involving an investigation of American society in the 20th century.

The first of these studies shows the relationship between corporations and crime, and accounts for the divergence between an 'imaginary social order' and the real activities of police, state and corporation. The second develops the idea of the underworld as servant – servant of the corporations and their local and national representatives.

'A landmark in the creation of a marxist criminology and a clear rebuttal of those socialists who would view crime as a marginal issue or a diversion from the concerns of marxist theory and practice.' Jock Young.